VOGUE KNITTING

STITCHIONARY 5

The Ultimate Stitch Dictionary from the Editors of Vogue Knitting Magazine

volume five
lace knitting

VOGUE® KNITTING
STITCHIONARY® 5

The Ultimate Stitch Dictionary from the Editors of Vogue® Knitting Magazine

volume five
lace knitting

sixth&spring books

sixth&spring books

161 Avenue of the Americas,
New York, New York 10013
sixthandspringbooks.com

Managing Editor
Wendy Williams

Vice President, Publisher
Trisha Malcolm

Senior Editor
Michelle Bredeson

Production Manager
David Joinnides

Book Editor
Carla Scott

Creative Director
Joe Vior

Art Director
Diane Lamphron

President
Art Joinnides

Graphic Designer
Becca Loewenberg

Patterns Editor
Joni Coniglio

Technical Editors
Lisa Buccellato
Lori Steinberg

Technical Illustrations
Uli Mönch

3   5   7   9   10   8   6   4   2
Manufactured in China
First Edition

Library of Congress Control Number: 2009941355
ISBN-10: 1-933027-93-2
ISBN-13: 978-1-933027-93-7

The patterns for the garments shown on the following pages are available for purchase at vogueknitting.com:
Page 9: Mesh Lace Tank, *Vogue Knitting,* Spring/Summer 2008
Page 29: Leaf Tank, *Vogue Knitting,* Spring/Summer 2008
Page 51: Feather and Fan Dress, *Vogue Knitting,* Spring/Summer 2009
Page 67: Medallion Top, *Vogue Knitting,* Spring/Summer 2008
Page 125: Lace Stockings, *Vogue Knitting,* Spring/Summer 2009
Page 141: Sideways Cardigan, *Vogue Knitting,* Spring/Summer 2008
Page 161: Botanica Medallion Cardi, *Vogue Knitting,* Spring/Summer 2009

Photo Credits:
Jack Deutsch: front cover, back cover and all swatches
Rose Callahan: pages 9, 29, 51 and 67
Paul Amato for LVARepresents.com: 125, 141 and 161

contents

We dedicate this book to all the wonderfully skilled knitters who spent their days (and nights) creating the beautiful swatches that appear in this book.

When we first conceived of the Stitchionary series, we envisioned a three-volume set. But while poring through the *Vogue Knitting* archives, we found that we had too many wonderful patterns to limit ourselves to just three books. In the fourth installment, we switched our focus to crochet, but for this fifth, we return to knitting and focus on lace.

A staple of knitting for hundreds of years, lace still makes appearances on the runway. It comes in many varieties—light and airy, chunky, simple, intricate—and is very versatile. You can incorporate lace into your knitted garments in various ways: Swap a plain stockinette stitch in a simple sweater for an allover lace pattern; add lace edgings to cuffs, collars and hems; design an entire shawl around a dramatic lace motif; design a lovely scarf by simply repeating a lace pattern as many times as you want. The possibilities are endless.

While lace knitting is often used as a general term to refer to stitches that include yarn overs, it is also used to distinguish it from knitted lace. Lace knitting and knitted lace—is there a difference? In fact there is. Lace knitting is single-sided, that is, the yarn overs and decreases are worked on one side only (the right side) while the alternate (wrong-side) rows are worked plain, as either knit or purl. In knitted lace the eyelet pattern is worked on every row. This book features both kinds of lace. Just remember when working ny type of lace, it is important to keep track of every stitch, because forgetting one yarn over will throw everything off. It is a good idea to count the stitches after every eyelet row to be sure you have the correct number, at least until you have a feel for the pattern.

We've divided the more than 150 lace patterns into seven chapters. Easy/Mesh patterns are the most straightforward and perfect for first-time lace knitters. The Allover patterns range from small and simple to fairly complex and challenging. In the Combos chapter, lace teams up with cables, embroidery and more to create exciting patterns. In the Edgings chapter, knitters will find the perfect finishing touch for any garment, while Motifs take center stage and

provide an excellent starting point for a design. Panels can stand alone or team up with other patterns to create stunning effects. Chevrons add movement and visual interest with their undulating rhythms.

Complete written instructions and charts are given for all of the lace patterns. While all skill levels are represented in this book, we hope knitters previously intimidated by lace will be inspired to challenge themselves and tackle more intricate lace patterns. So grab your needles and join the timeless tradition of lace knitting.

Carla Scott

trefoil p. 140

how to use this book

Vogue Knitting Stitchionary, Volume 5: Lace Knitting is divided into seven chapters: Easy/Mesh, Edgings, Chevrons, Allover, Panels, Combos and Motifs. As in the previous edition, we arranged the stitches in each chapter in order of difficulty, from the easiest to the most challenging. In naming some swatches we used the most commonly recognized or descriptive names, while for others we just had fun in determining a title.

In order to accommodate your knitting preferences, we have used written instructions as well as charts to explain each stitch. All of the instructions use the *Vogue Knitting* style, with standard knitting abbreviations, easy-to-understand terminology and the internationally recognized stitch symbols for the charts. References to special techniques used in the stitch, such as cables, are spelled out at the beginning of each set of instructions, so you do not have to flip back to a glossary to find the meaning.

We knit the swatches using Zarina from Filatura Di Crosa—an extra-fine 100-percent merino wool. This yarn is ideal for showing off the intricate details of lace. Most of the time, we used a background of stockinette stitches, which are not included in the instructions. We used sizes 3–4 (3.25–3.5mm) needles to knit the swatches. Note that if you use a different weight yarn or a textured yarn or different-sized needles, the resulting look of the lace stitch pattern may be different than what we show.

Always remember to make a gauge swatch with the yarn you are using for the project. This will make you familiar with the pattern stitch and you will know if that particular stitch worked well with the desired yarn. Because lace is so textured, it is best to use a more basic yarn to illuminate the pattern. Using a highly textured yarn may hide the inherent features of the lace. And please note that some stitches are continuous, with pattern repeats, and some are panels that can be inserted into a design or combined with other stitches.

easy/mesh

1 dotted ribs

(multiple of 4 sts plus 3)
Rows 1, 3, 5 and 7 (RS) *P3, k1; rep from *, end p3.
Rows 2, 4 and 6 K3, *p1, k3; rep from * to end.
Row 8 K1, yo, k2tog, *p1, k1, yo, k2tog; rep from * to end.
Rep rows 1–8.

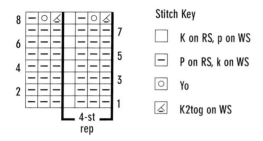

Stitch Key

☐ K on RS, p on WS

⊟ P on RS, k on WS

○ Yo

◹ K2tog on WS

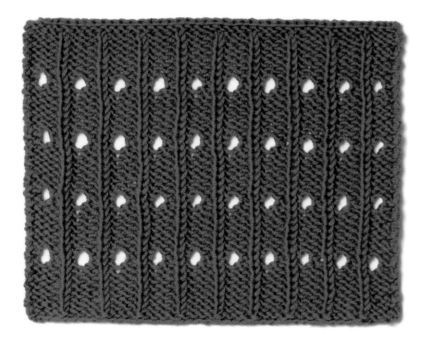

2 snowballs

(multiple of 8 sts plus 1)
Row 1 (RS) *P1, k3; rep from *, end p1.
Rows 2, 4 and 6 K1, *p3, k1; rep from * to end.
Row 3 *P1, k2tog, yo, k1, p1, k3; rep from *, end p1.
Row 5 Rep row 1.
Row 7 *P1, k3, p1, k2tog, yo, k1; rep from *, end p1.
Row 8 Rep row 2.
Rep rows 1–8.

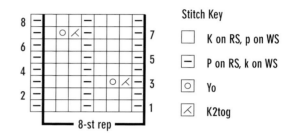

Stitch Key

☐ K on RS, p on WS

⊟ P on RS, k on WS

○ Yo

◹ K2tog

3 raindrops

(multiple of 8 sts plus 7)
Row 1 (RS) P2, *ssk, yo, [k1, p1] 3 times;
rep from * to last 5 sts, end ssk, yo, k1, p2.
Rows 2 and 4 K2, p1, k1, p1, *k5, p1, k1,
p1; rep from *, end k2.
Row 3 P2, *[K1, p1] twice, k3, p1; rep from
* to last 5 sts, end [k1, p1] twice, p1.

Row 5 P2, *k1, p1; rep from * to last 3 sts,
end k1, p2.
Row 6 K2, *p1, k1; rep from * to last 3 sts,
end p1, k2.
Row 7 P2, *[K1, p1] twice, ssk, yo, k1, p1;
rep from * to last 5 sts, end [k1, p1] twice, p1.

Rows 8 and 10 K6, *p1, k1, p1, k5; rep from *,
end k1.
Row 9 P2, *k3, [p1, k1] twice, p1; rep from *
to last 5 sts, end k3, p2.
Row 11 Rep row 5.
Row 12 Rep row 6.
Rep rows 1–12.

easy/mesh

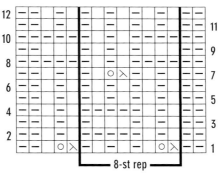

8-st rep

Stitch Key

☐ K on RS, p on WS

— P on RS, k on WS

○ Yo

⧄ Ssk

4 string of pearls

(multiple of 14 sts plus 3)
Row 1 (RS) K1, *k5, k2tog, yo, k1, yo, ssk, k4; rep from *, end k2.
Rows 2 and 4 Purl.
Row 3 K1, *k3, k2tog, yo, k5, yo, ssk, k2; rep from *, end k2.
Row 5 K1, *k1, k2tog, yo, k9, yo, ssk; rep from *, end k2.
Row 6 Purl.
Rep rows 1–6.

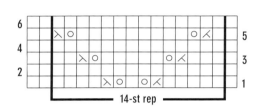

Stitch Key

☐ K on RS, p on WS

⊙ Yo

⟋ K2tog

⟍ Ssk

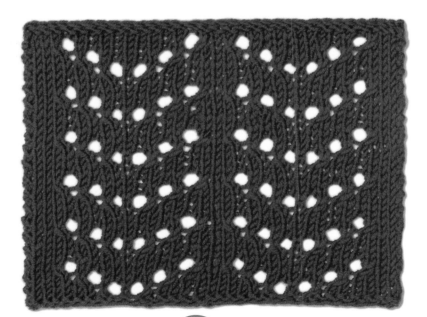

5 field of diamonds

(worked over an even number of sts)
Row 1 (RS) K1, *k2tog, yo; rep from *, end k1.
Rows 2, 4 and 6 K1, p to last st, k1.
Rows 3 and 7 Knit.
Row 5 K1, *yo, k2tog; rep from *, end k1.
Row 8 Rep row 2.
Rep rows 1–8.

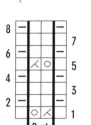

Stitch Key

☐ K on RS, p on WS

— K on WS

⊙ Yo

⟋ K2tog

6 stars and stripes

(worked over an odd number of sts)
Row 1 (RS) Knit.
Rows 2 and 4 Knit.
Row 3 *K2tog, yo; rep from *, end k1.
Row 5 Knit.
Row 6 Purl.
Rep rows 1–6.

Stitch Key

	K on RS, p on WS
−	K on WS
○	Yo
⟋	K2tog

7 polka dots

(worked over an odd number of sts)
Row 1 (WS) Knit.
Rows 2 and 4 Knit.
Row 3 K1, p1, *yo, p2tog; rep from *, end k1.
Rep rows 1–4.

Stitch Key

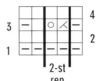

	K on RS, p on WS
−	K on WS
○	Yo
⟋	P2tog on WS

6

7

8 sea foam

(multiple of 10 sts plus 8)
Rows 1 and 2 Knit.
Row 3 (RS) K7, *yo twice, k1, yo 3 times, k1, yo 4 times, k1, yo 3 times, k1, yo twice, k6; rep from *, end k1.
Row 4 Knit, dropping all yos off LH needle without working them.
Rows 5 and 6 Knit.
Row 7 K2, then rep from * of row 3 to last 6 sts, end yo twice, k1, yo 3 times, k1, yo 4 times, k1, yo 3 times, k1, yo twice, k2.
Row 8 Knit, dropping all yos off LH needle without working them.
Rep rows 1–8.

Stitch Key

☐ K on RS

☐ K on WS

▭ [Yo] twice, k1, [yo] 3 times, k1, [yo] 4 times, k1, [yo] 3 times, k1, [yo] twice

NOTE On WS rows above yos, drop yos off LH needle without working them.

9 at an angle

(worked over an even number of sts)
Row 1 (RS) K1, *yo, ssk; rep from *, end k1.
Row 2 K1, p to last st, k1.
Rep rows 1–2.

Stitch Key

☐ K on RS, p on WS

☐ K on WS

◯ Yo

⧄ Ssk

8

9

14

10 a different slant

(worked over an even number of sts)
Row 1 (RS) K1, *k2tog, yo; rep from *, end k1.
Row 2 K1, p to last st, k1.
Rep rows 1–2.

Stitch Key

☐ K on RS, p on WS

— K on WS

○ Yo

⊠ K2tog

11 millipedes

(multiple of 10 sts plus 1)
Row 1 (RS) *K2, ssk, [k1, yo] twice,
k1, k2tog, k1; rep from *, end k1.
Row 2 Purl.
Rep rows 1–2.

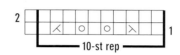

Stitch Key

☐ K on RS, p on WS

○ Yo

⊠ K2tog

⊠ Ssk

10

11

12 gingerbread crumbs

(worked over an even number of sts)
Row 1 (RS) K1, *yo, ssk; rep from *, end k1.
Rows 2 and 4 K1, p to last st, k1.
Row 3 K1, *ssk, yo; rep from *, end k1.
Rep rows 1–4.

Stitch Key

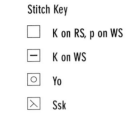

☐ K on RS, p on WS

— K on WS

◯ Yo

╲ Ssk

13 twisted trellis

(worked over an even number of sts)
Row 1 (RS) K1, *yo, k2tog; rep from *, end k1.
Row 2 P1, *yo, p2tog; rep from *, end p1.
Rep rows 1–2.

Stitch Key

☐ K on RS, p on WS

◯ Yo

╱ K2tog on RS, p2tog on WS

12

13

14 uphill

(multiple of 3 sts plus 2)
Row 1 (RS) K2, *k1, ssk, yo; rep from *, end k3.
Rows 2 and 4 K1, p to last st, k1.
Row 3 K2, *ssk, yo, k1; rep from * to end.
Row 5 K1, *ssk, yo, k1; rep from *, end k1.
Row 6 Rep row 2.
Rep rows 1–6.

Stitch Key

☐ K on RS, p on WS

▬ K on WS

◉ Yo

◩ Ssk

3-st rep

15 downhill

(multiple of 3 sts plus 2)
Row 1 (RS) K3, *yo, k2tog, k1; rep from *, end k2.
Rows 2 and 4 K1, p to last st, k1.
Row 3 *K1, yo, k2tog; rep from *, end k2.
Row 5 K2, *yo, k2tog, k1; rep from * to end.
Row 6 Rep row 2.
Rep rows 1–6.

Stitch Key

☐ K on RS, p on WS

▬ K on WS

◉ Yo

◪ K2tog

3-st rep

easy/mesh

16 crab walk

(multiple of 7 sts plus 2)
Row 1 (RS) K1, *k1, k2tog, yo, k1, yo, ssk, k1; rep from *, end k1.
Rows 2 and 4 Purl.
Row 3 K1, *k2tog, yo, k3, yo, ssk; rep from *, end k1.
Rep rows 1–4.

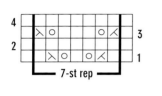

Stitch Key

☐ K on RS, p on WS

◯ Yo

◿ K2tog

◺ Ssk

17 twist and turn

(worked over an odd number of sts)
Row 1 (RS) K1, *yo, k2tog; rep from * to end.
Rows 2 and 4 Purl.
Row 3 *Ssk, yo; rep from *, end k1.
Rep rows 1–4.

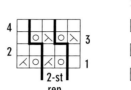

Stitch Key

☐ K on RS, p on WS

◯ Yo

◿ K2tog

◺ Ssk

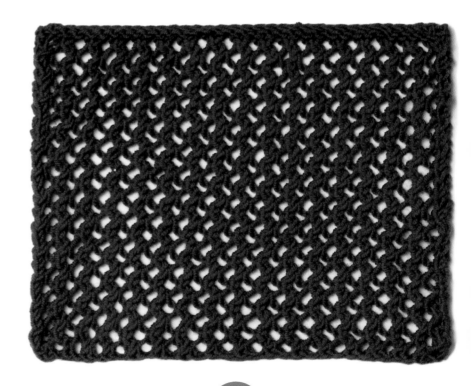

16

17

18 stained glass windows

(multiple of 7 sts plus 3)
Row 1 (RS) K2tog, yo, k1, *yo, ssk,
[k2tog, yo] twice, k1; rep from * to end.
Rows 2 and 4 Purl.
Row 3 *K1, [yo, ssk] twice, k2tog, yo;
rep from *, end k1, yo, ssk.
Rep rows 1–4.

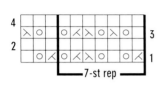

Stitch Key

☐ K on RS, p on WS

◯ Yo

╱ K2tog

╲ Ssk

19 between the lines

(multiple of 6 sts plus 1)
Row 1 (RS) *K1, yo, k1, SK2P,
k1, yo; rep from *, end k1.
Row 2 Knit.
Rep rows 1–2.

easy/mesh

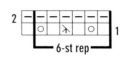

Stitch Key

☐ K on RS

─ K on WS

◯ Yo

⋊ SK2P

20 cobblestones

(multiple of 6 sts plus 5)
Row 1 (RS) K1, *k3, yo, SK2P, yo; rep from *, end k4.
Row 2 K1, p to last st, k1.
Row 3 K1, *yo, SK2P, yo, k3; rep from *, end last rep k1 (instead of k3).
Row 4 Rep row 2.
Rep rows 1–4.

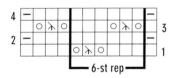

Stitch Key

□	K on RS, p on WS
—	K on WS
○	Yo
⋏	SK2P

21 fairy wings

(multiple of 4 sts plus 3)
Row 1 (RS) K1, *yo, SK2P, yo, k1; rep from * to last 2 sts, end yo, ssk.
Rows 2 and 4 Purl.
Row 3 K2tog, yo, *k1, yo, SK2P, yo; rep from *, end k1.
Rep rows 1–4.

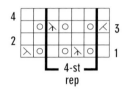

Stitch Key

□	K on RS, p on WS
○	Yo
⟋	K2tog
⟍	Ssk
⋏	SK2P

20

21

22 broken checkerboard

(multiple of 6 sts plus 1)
Rows 1 and 3 (WS) K2, *p3, k3; rep from *, end last rep k2 (instead of k3).
Row 2 P2, *k3, p3; rep from *, end last rep p2 (instead of p3).

Row 4 K2, *yo, SK2P, yo, k3; rep from * end last rep k2 (instead of k3).
Rows 5 and 7 Rep row 2.
Row 6 Rep row 1.
Row 8 K2tog, yo, *k3, yo, SK2P, yo; rep from * to last 5 sts, end k3, yo, ssk.
Rep rows 1–8.

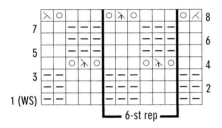

Stitch Key

☐	K on RS, p on WS
—	P on RS, k on WS
○	Yo
╱	K2tog
╲	Ssk
⋏	SK2P

23 wildflower meadow

(multiple of 8 sts plus 7)
Row 1 (RS) K1, *yo, k2tog, k1, ssk, yo, k3; rep from *, end last rep k1 (instead of 3).
Rows 2 and 4 Purl.
Row 3 K1, *k1, yo, S2KP, yo; rep from *, end k2.
Rep rows 1–4.

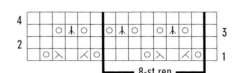

Stitch Key

☐	K on RS, p on WS
○	Yo
╱	K2tog
╲	Ssk
⋏	S2KP

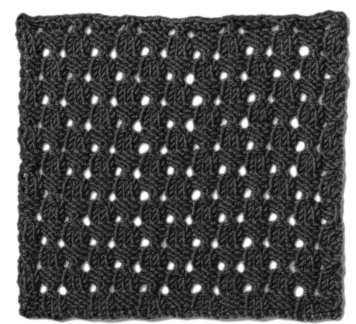

22

23

24 hens and chicks

(multiple of 8 sts plus 7)
Row 1 (RS) K2tog, yo twice, *k3tog, yo twice, ssk, k1, k2tog, yo twice; rep from * to last 5 sts, end k3tog, yo twice, ssk.
Rows 2 and 4 Purl, working [p1, k1] into each double yo.

Row 3 K1, yo, ssk, *k1, k2tog, yo twice, k3tog, yo twice, ssk; rep from * to last 4 sts, end k1, k2tog, yo, k1.
Rep rows 1–4.

Stitch Key

□	K on RS, p on WS
—	K on WS
○	Yo
⟋	K2tog
⟍	Ssk
⟰	K3tog

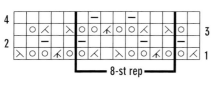

25 jumping jacks

(multiple of 9 sts plus 7)
Row 1 (RS) K3, k2tog, *yo twice, SK2P; rep from * to last 5 sts, end yo twice, k2tog, k3.
Rows 2 and 4 Knit, working [p1, k1] into each double yo.
Row 3 K6, *k2tog, yo twice, ssk, k5; rep from *, end k1.

Row 5 K5, *k2tog, yo, k2, yo, ssk, k3; rep from *, end k2.
Row 6 Knit.
Row 7 K4, *k2tog, yo, k4, yo, ssk, k1; rep from *, end k3.
Row 8 Knit.
Rep rows 1–8.

Stitch Key

□	K on RS, p on WS
—	K on WS
○	Yo
⟋	K2tog
⟍	Ssk
⟰	SK2P

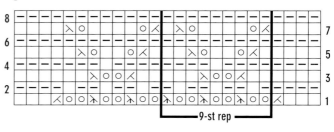

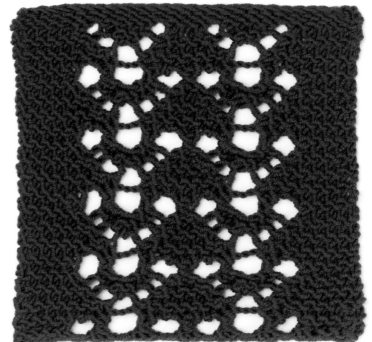

26 bubble 'n' squeak

(multiple of 6 sts plus 2)
Note On rows 4 and 8, work double yos of preceding row as 2 separate sts.
Row 1 (RS) P1, *p1, yo, ssk, k2tog, yo, p1; rep from *, end p1.
Row 2 K1, *k1, p4, k1; rep from *, end k1.
Row 3 P1, *p1, k2tog, yo twice, ssk, p1; rep from *, end p1.
Row 4 K1, *k1, p2, k1, p1, k1; rep from *, end k1.
Row 5 P1, *k2tog, yo, p2, yo, ssk; rep from *, end p1.
Row 6 K1, *p2, k2, p2; rep from *, end k1.
Row 7 P1, *yo, ssk, p2, k2tog, yo; rep from *, end p1.
Row 8 K1, *k1, p1, k2, p2; rep from *, end k1.
Rep rows 1–8.

Stitch Key

- ☐ K on RS, p on WS
- ▭ P on RS, k on WS
- ○ Yo
- ⊠ K2tog
- ⊠ Ssk

6-st rep

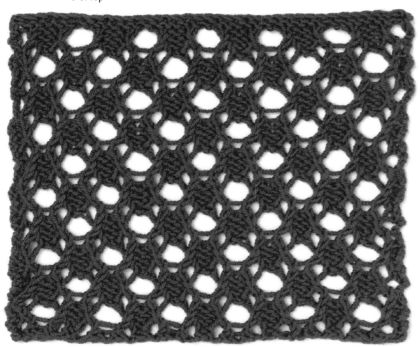

27 lovely lattice

(multiple of 3 sts plus 1)
Row 1 (RS) K2, *SK2P, yo twice; rep from * to last 2 sts, end k2.
Row 2 K2, *p1 in first yo, k1 in 2nd yo, p1; rep from * to last 2 sts, end k2.
Row 3 Knit.
Row 4 (WS) Rep row 1.
Row 5 Rep row 2.
Row 6 Rep row 3.
Rep rows 1–6.

Stitch Key

- ☐ K on RS, p on WS
- ▭ P on RS, k on WS
- ○ Yo
- ⋌ SK2P on RS
- ⋋ SK2P on WS

3-st rep

easy/mesh

28 ducks in a row

(worked over an even number of sts)
Row 1 (RS) Knit.
Row 2 K1, *p2tog, yo; rep from *, end k1.
Row 3 K1, *p1, then [p1, k1] into next st; with tip of LH needle,
pass 3rd st on RH needle (the p st) over first 2 sts and off
needle; rep from *, end k1.
Row 4 K1, p to last st, k1.
Rep rows 1–4.

Stitch Key

☐ K on RS, p on WS

▬ K on WS

○ Yo

╱ P2tog on WS

⧖ P1, [p1, k1] into next st; with tip of
LH needle, pass 3rd st on RH needle
(the p st) over first 2 sts and off
needle

29 starry night

(multiple of 6 sts)
Row 1 (RS) *Sl 1 knitwise, k2, psso the k2, k3; rep from * to end.
Row 2 *P4, yo, p1; rep from * to end.
Row 3 *K3, sl 1 knitwise, k2, psso the k2; rep from * to end.
Row 4 *P1, yo, p4; rep from * to end.
Rep rows 1–4.

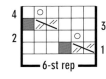

Stitch Key

☐ K on RS, p on WS

○ Yo

⧖ Sl 1 knitwise, k2, psso the k2

▨ No stitch

30 periwinkles

(multiple of 6 sts plus 2)
Row 1 (RS) K1, *k4, k2tog, yo; rep from *, end k1.
Row 2 P1, *yo, p1, p2tog, p3; rep from *, end p1.
Row 3 K1, *k2, k2tog, k2, yo; rep from *, end k1.
Row 4 P1, *yo, p3, p2tog, p1; rep from *, end p1.
Row 5 K1, *k2tog, k4, yo; rep from *, end k1.
Row 6 P2, *p4, yo, p2tog; rep from * to end.
Row 7 K1, *k1, yo, k3, k2tog; rep from *, end k1.
Row 8 P1, *p2tog, p2, yo, p2; rep from *, end p1.
Row 9 K1, *k3, yo, k1, k2tog; rep from *, end k1.
Row 10 P1, *p2tog, yo, p4; rep from *, end p1.
Rep rows 1–10.

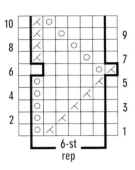

Stitch Key

☐ K on RS, p on WS

⊡ Yo

⊠ K2tog on RS, p2tog on WS

30

31 flying saucers

1/1 RT Bring RH needle in front of first st on LH needle and k 2nd st, but do not remove it from needle; then k first st and sl both sts from needle.

1/1 LT Bring RH needle behind first st on LH needle and to front between first and 2nd sts; k 2nd st but do not remove it from needle; bring RH needle to right and in front of first st and k first st, then sl both sts from needle.

(multiple of 6 sts plus 2)

Row 1 (RS) K1, *p2, 1/1 LT, p2; rep from *, end k1.

Row 2 K1, *k2, p2, k2; rep from *, end k1.

Row 3 K1, *k3tog, yo, SK2P; rep from * end k1.

Row 4 K1, *p1, [k1, p1] twice into yo, p1; rep from *, end k1.

Row 5 K2, *p4, 1/1 RT; rep from *, end last rep k2 (instead of 1/1 RT).

Row 6 K1, p1, *k4, p2; rep from *, end last rep p1,

k1 (instead of p2).

Row 7 K1, yo, SK2P, *k3tog, yo, SK2P; rep from *, end last rep k1 (instead of SK2P).

Row 8 K1, [k1, p1] into yo, p1, *p1, [k1, p1] twice into yo, p1; rep from * to last 3 sts, end p1, [k1, p1] into yo, k1.

Rep rows 1–8.

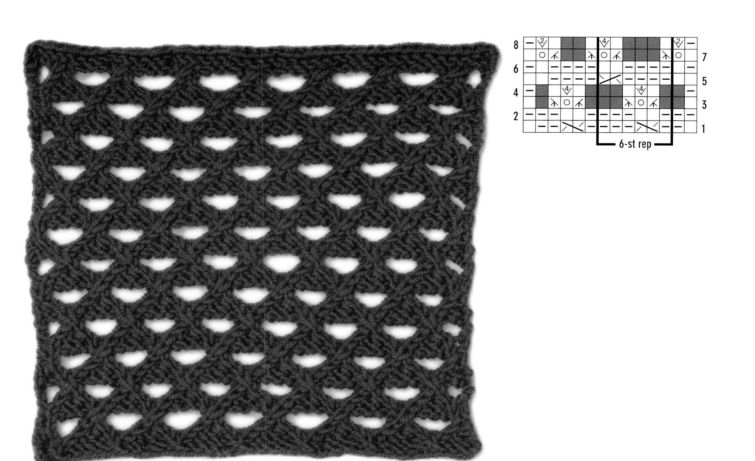

Stitch Key

☐ K on RS, p on WS

⊟ P on RS, k on WS

○ Yo

K3tog

SK2P

[k1, p1] into yo

[k1, p1] twice into yo

1/1 RT

1/1 LT

▧ No stitch

6-st rep

32 bed of roses

(multiple of 6 sts plus 1)
Row 1 (RS) *K2, yo, k3tog, yo, k1; rep from * to last st, end k1.
Row 2 K1, *p2tog, yo, p1, yo, p2tog, p1; rep from *, end last rep k1 (instead of p1).

Row 3 K5, *yo, k3tog, yo, k3; rep from * to last 2 sts, end k2.
Row 4 K1, *yo, p2tog, p1, p2tog, yo, p1; rep from *, end last rep k1 (instead of p1).
Rep rows 1–4.

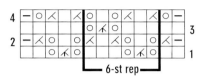

Stitch Key

☐   K on RS, p on WS

−   K on WS

◯   Yo

◩   P2tog on WS

⩘   K3tog on RS

33 shetland bead lace

(multiple of 6 sts plus 5)
Row 1 (WS) K3, *k2tog, yo, k1, yo, k2tog, k1; rep from *, end k2.
Row 2 K2, k2tog, yo, k3, *yo, SK2P, yo, k3; rep from * to last 4 sts, end yo, k2tog, k2.
Row 3 K3, *yo, k2tog, k1, k2tog, yo, k1; rep from *, end k2.
Row 4 K1, k2tog, yo, *k1, yo, SK2P, yo, k2; rep from * to last 8 sts, end k1, yo, SK2P, yo, k1, yo, k2tog, k1.
Rep rows 1–4.

Stitch Key

☐	K on RS, p on WS
—	K on WS
○	Yo
◿	K2tog on WS
◺	K2tog on RS
⊼	SK2P

33

28

edgings

(worked over an even number of sts)
Rows 1, 3 and 7 (RS) Knit.
Rows 2, 4 and 6 K1, p to last st, k1.
Row 5 K1, *k2tog, yo; rep from *, end k1.
Row 8 Rep row 2.
Bind off. Run a length of ribbon through eyelets on row 5.

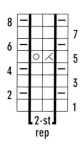

Stitch Key

☐ K on RS, p on WS

— K on WS

○ Yo

╱ K2tog

Cluster st Wyif, [sl next st dropping extra 2 yos] 5 times, [bring yarn to back between needles, sl 5 sts back to LH needle, bring yarn to front between needles, sl 5 sts to RH needle] twice.
(multiple of 6 sts plus 1)
Row 1 (WS) Knit.
Row 2 K1, *[k1 wrapping yarn 3 times around needle (instead of once)] 5 times, k1; rep from * to end.
Row 3 K1, *work Cluster st over 5 sts, k1; rep from * to end.
Rows 4 and 5 Knit.

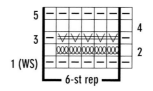

Stitch Key

☐ K on RS, p on WS

— K on WS

▨ K1, wrapping yarn 3 times around needle (instead of once)

⩒⩒⩒⩒⩒ Cluster stitch

36 falling snow

(multiple of 6 sts plus 1)
Row 1 (RS) *K1, p1, k1, p2tog, yo, p1; rep from *, end k1.
Rows 2, 4 and 6 P1, *k1, p1; rep from * to end.
Rows 3 and 7 *K1, p1; rep from *, end k1.
Row 5 *K1, p1, yo, p2tog, k1, p1; rep from *, end k1.
Row 8 Rep row 2.
Rep rows 1–8.

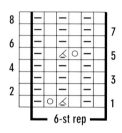

Stitch Key

☐ K on RS, p on WS

— P on RS, k on WS

⊡ Yo

◹ P2tog

37 eyelet ribs

(multiple of 4 sts plus 1)
Row 1 (RS) *K1, p1; rep from *, end k1.
Row 2 P1, *k1, yo, k2tog, p1; rep from * to end.
Rep rows 1–2.

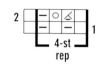

Stitch Key

☐ K on RS, p on WS

— P on RS, k on WS

⊡ Yo

◹ K2tog on WS

edgings

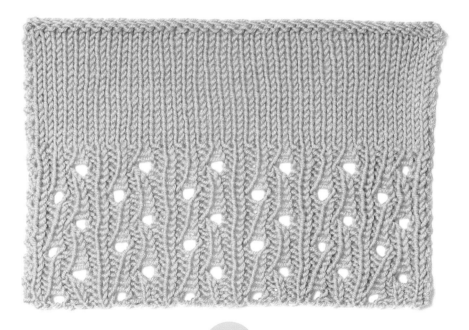

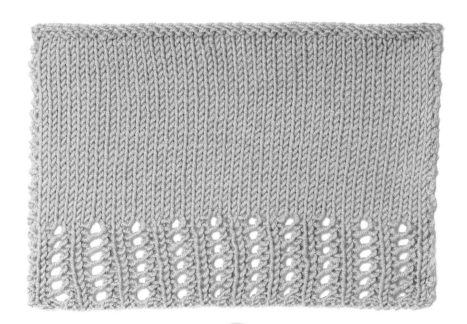

(multiple of 10 sts plus 5)

Rows 1 and 3 (RS) *P2, k1 tbl, p2; rep from * to end.

Row 2 *K2, p1 tbl, k2; rep from * to end.

Row 4 K2, p1 tbl, k2, *cable cast on 8 sts, k2, p1 tbl, k2; rep from * to end.

Row 5 P2, k1 tbl, p2, *k8 tbl, p2, k1 tbl, p2; rep from * to end.

Row 6 K2, p1 tbl, k2, *p2tog, p6, k2, p1 tbl, k2; rep from * to end.

Row 7 P2, k1 tbl, p2, *k7, p2, k1 tbl, p2; rep from * to end.

Row 8 K2, p1 tbl, k2, *p2tog, p5, k2, p1 tbl, k2; rep from * to end.

Row 9 P2, k1 tbl, p2, *k6, p2, k1 tbl, p2; rep from * to end.

Row 10 K2, p1 tbl, k2, *p2tog, p4, k2, p1 tbl, k2; rep from * to end.

Row 11 P2, k1 tbl, p2, *k5, p2, k1 tbl, p2; rep from * to end.

Row 12 K2, p1 tbl, k2, *p2tog, p3, k2, p1 tbl, k2; rep from * to end.

Row 13 P2, k1 tbl, p2, *k4, p2, k1 tbl, p2; rep from * to end.

Row 14 K2, p1 tbl, k2, *p2tog, p2, k2, p1 tbl, k2; rep from * to end.

Row 15 P2, k1 tbl, p2, *k3, p2, k1 tbl, p2; rep from * to end.

Row 16 K2, p1 tbl, k2, *p2tog, p1, k2, p1 tbl, k2; rep from * to end.

Row 17 P2, k1 tbl, p2, *k2, p2, k1 tbl, p2; rep from * to end.

Row 18 K2, p1 tbl, k2, *p2tog, k2, p1 tbl, k2; rep from * to end.

Row 19 *P2, k1 tbl, p1, p2tog; rep from *, end p2, k1 tbl, p2.

Rep rows 2–19 once more.

Row 20 K2, p1 tbl, k2, *k7, p1 tbl, k2; rep from * to end.

Row 21 P2, k1 tbl, p2, *p7, k1 tbl, p2; rep from * to end.

Row 22 K2, p1 tbl, k2, *k2, p1, k4, p1 tbl, k2; rep from * to end.

Row 23 P2, k1 tbl, p2, *p1, k3, p3, k1 tbl, p2; rep from * to end.

Row 24 K2, p1 tbl, k2, *p5, k2, p1 tbl, k2; rep from * to end.

Row 25 K1, p3, k1, *k6, p3, k1; rep from * to end.

Row 26 P2, k1, p2, *p7, k1, p2; rep from * to end.

Row 27 Knit.

Row 28 Purl.

Stitch Key

☐ K on RS, p on WS

— P on RS, k on WS

⊠ P2tog on WS

⊠ P2tog on RS

Ⓠ K1 tbl on RS, p1 tbl on WS

⊂ Cable cast on 1 st

▦ No stitch

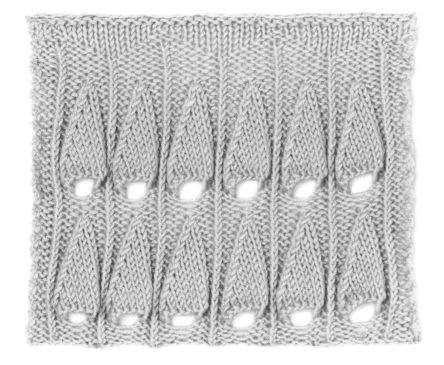

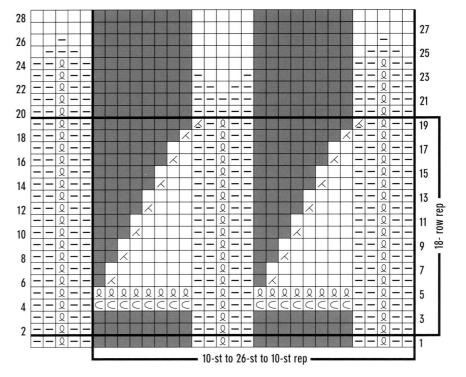

(multiple of 10 sts plus 3)
Row 1 (RS) K1, *k1, yo, k3, SK2P, k3, yo; rep from *, end k2.
Rows 2, 4 and 6 K1, p to last st, k1.
Row 3 K1, *k2, yo, k2, SK2P, k2, yo, k1; rep from *, end k2.
Row 5 K1, k2tog, *[yo, k1] twice, SK2P, [k1, yo] twice, SK2P; rep from *, end last rep k2tog, k1 (instead of SK2P).
Row 7 K2, *yo, p2tog; rep from *, end k1.
Row 8 Knit.

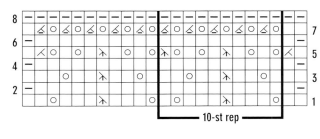

Stitch Key

☐ K on RS, p on WS

— P on RS, k on WS

▢ Yo

◿ K2tog

◿ P2tog

↗ SK2P

edgings

(multiple of 11 sts)
Row 1 (RS) *K5, yo, k4, SKP; rep from * to end.
Rows 2, 4, 6 and 8 Purl.
Row 3 *K2tog, k3, yo, k1, yo, k3, SKP; rep from * to end.
Row 5 *K2tog, k2, yo, k1, yo, SKP, yo, k2, SKP; rep from * to end.
Row 7 *K2tog, [k1, yo] twice, [SKP, yo] twice, k1, SKP; rep from * to end.
Row 10 Purl.
Rep rows 1–10.

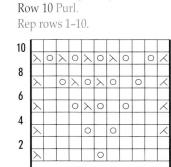

Stitch Key

☐ K on RS, p on WS

▢ Yo

◿ K2tog

◺ SKP

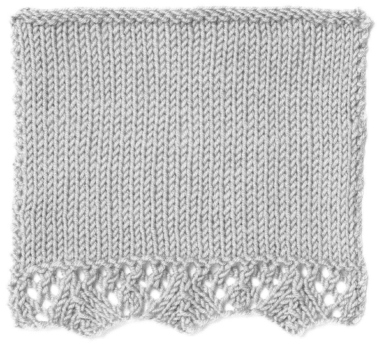

39

40

(begin with a multiple of 16 sts plus 1)

Row 1 (RS) Knit.

Row 2 and all WS rows Purl.

Rows 3 and 5 K1, *k1, yo, S2KP, yo, k1; rep from *, end k1.

Row 7 K1, *k2, yo, ssk, yo, k2, yo, S2KP, yo, k2, yo, k2tog, yo, k3; rep from * to end.

Row 9 Knit.

Row 11 K1, *[yo, k1] twice, yo, k3, ssk, S2KP, k2tog, k3, [yo, k1] 3 times; rep from * to end.

Row 13 Knit.

Row 15 K1, *[yo, k1] 4 times, [ssk] twice, S2KP, [k2tog] twice, k1, [yo, k1] 4 times; rep from * to end.

Row 17 Knit.

Row 19 K1, *[yo, k1] 5 times, [ssk] twice, S2KP, [k2tog] twice, k1, [yo, k1] 5 times; rep from * to end.

Row 21 Knit.

Row 23 K1, *[Yo, k1] 5 times, yo, [ssk] 3 times, S2KP, [k2tog] 3 times, [yo, k1] 6 times; rep from * to end.

Row 25 Knit.

Row 27 K1, *[yo, k1] 5 times, yo, k2, [ssk] 3 times, S2KP, [k2tog] 3 times, k2, [yo, k1] 6 times; rep from * to end.

Row 29 Knit.

Row 31 K1, *[yo, k1] 7 times, [ssk] 4 times, S2KP, [k2tog] 4 times, k1, [yo, k1] 7 times; rep from * to end.

Row 33 Knit.

Row 35 K1, *[yo, k1] 6 times, yo, k3, [ssk] 4 times, S2KP, [k2tog] 4 times, k3, [yo, k1] 7 times; rep from * to end.

Row 37 Knit.

Row 39 P1, *M1 purl, p10, M1 purl, p11; rep from * to end.

Row 41 Purl.

Bind off loosely.

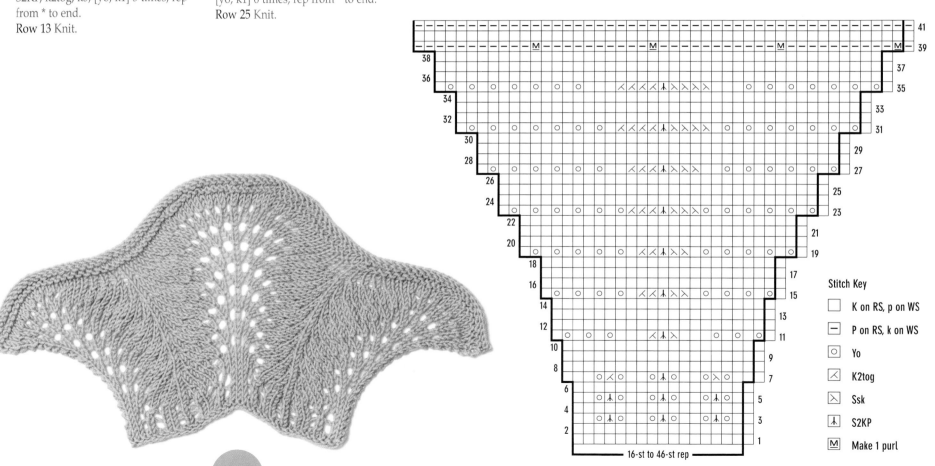

Stitch Key

☐	K on RS, p on WS
—	P on RS, k on WS
○	Yo
⟋	K2tog
⟍	Ssk
⋏	S2KP
M	Make 1 purl

16-st to 46-st rep

edgings

(multiple of 17 sts plus 1)

Row 1 (RS) *K10, yo, k1, yo, k3, SK2P; rep from *, end k1.

Row 2 and all WS rows Purl.

Row 3 *K11, yo, k1, yo, k2, SK2P; rep from *, end k1.

Row 5 *K1, k3tog, k4, yo, k1, yo, k3, [yo, k1] twice, SK2P; rep from *, end k1.

Row 7 *K1, k3tog, k3, yo, k1, yo, k9; rep from *, end k1.

Row 9 *K1, k3tog, k2, yo, k1, yo, k10; rep from *, end k1.

Row 11 *K1, k3tog, [k1, yo] twice, k3, yo, k1, yo, k4, SK2P; rep from *, end k1.

Row 12 Purl.

Rep rows 1–12 once more.

Rows 13–16 Rep rows 1–4.

Row 17 *K12, [yo, k1] twice, SK2P; rep from *, end k1.

Row 18 Purl.

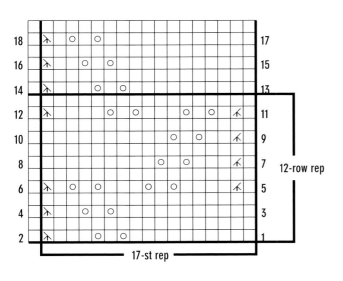

17-st rep

Stitch Key

☐ K on RS, p on WS

⊙ Yo

⊼ K3tog

⋏ SK2P

(multiple of 20 sts plus 3)

Row 1 (RS) K1, *[k1 tbl, p2] 3 times, k1 tbl, yo, k1, yo, [k1 tbl, p2] 3 times; rep from *, end k1 tbl, k1.

Row 2 P1, *[p1 tbl, k2] 3 times, p1 tbl, p3, [p1 tbl, k2] 3 times; rep from *, end p1 tbl, p1.

Row 3 K1, *[k1 tbl, p2] 3 times, k1 tbl, yo, k3, yo, [k1 tbl, p2] 3 times; rep from *, end k1 tbl, k1.

Row 4 P1, *[p1 tbl, k2] 3 times, p1 tbl, p5, [p1 tbl, k2] 3 times; rep from *, end p1 tbl, p1.

Row 5 K1, *[k1 tbl, p2] 3 times, k1 tbl, yo, k2, yo, k2tog, k1, yo, [k1 tbl, p2] 3 times; rep from *, end k1 tbl, k1.

Row 6 P1, *[p1 tbl, k2] 3 times, p1 tbl, p7, [p1 tbl, k2] 3 times; rep from *, end p1 tbl, p1.

Row 7 K1, *[k1 tbl, p2tog] 3 times, k1 tbl, yo, k2, [yo, k2tog] twice, k1, yo, [k1 tbl, p2tog] 3 times; rep from *, end k1 tbl, k1.

Row 8 P1, *[p1 tbl, k1] 3 times, p1 tbl, p9, [p1 tbl, k1] 3 times; rep from *, end p1 tbl, p1.

Row 9 K1, *[k1 tbl, p1] 3 times, k1 tbl, yo, k4, yo, k2tog, k3, yo, [k1 tbl, p1] 3 times; rep from *, end k1 tbl, k1.

Row 10 P1, *[p1 tbl, k1] 3 times, p1 tbl, p11, [p1 tbl, k1] 3 times; rep from *, end p1 tbl, p1.

Row 11 K1, *[k2tog tbl] 3 times, k1 tbl, yo, k11, yo, [k2tog tbl] 3 times; rep from *, end k1 tbl, k1.

Row 12 P1, *k4, p13, k3; rep from *, end k1, p1.

Rep rows 1–12 twice more.

Stitch Key

☐ K on RS, p on WS

— P on RS, k on WS

○ Yo

╱ K2tog

╱ P2tog

ℚ K1 tbl on RS, p1 tbl on WS

╲ K2tog tbl

■ No stitch

44 petite scallops

(begin on 12 sts)
Note Sts for St st portion were picked up after edging was knit.
Row 1 (RS) K5, yo, k2tog, k5.
Row 2 [K2tog, yo twice] twice, k3, yo, k2tog, k1, p2—14 sts.
Row 3 K5, yo, k2tog, [k1, k1 into first yo, p1 into 2nd yo] twice, k1.
Row 4 [K2tog, yo twice] twice, k5, yo, k2tog, k1, p2—16 sts.
Row 5 K5, yo, k2tog, k3, [k1 into first yo, p1 into 2nd yo, k1] twice.
Row 6 [K2tog, yo twice] twice, k7, yo, k2tog, k1, p2—18 sts.
Row 7 K5, yo, k2tog, k5, [k1 into first yo, p1 into 2nd yo, k1] twice.
Row 8 Bind off 6 sts knitwise, k6, yo, k2tog, k1, p2—12 sts.
Rep rows 1–8.

Stitch Key

☐ K on RS, p on WS

— P on RS, k on WS

○ Yo

◹ K2tog on RS

◸ K2tog on WS

⌒ Bind off 1 st knitwise

12 to 18 to 12 sts

45 piecrust

(begin on 10 sts)
Notes 1) Sl sts at beg of RS rows purlwise wyif. 2) On row 2, work multiple yo as 4 separate sts.
3) Sts for St st portion were picked up after edging was knit.
Set-up row (WS) Knit.
Row 1 (RS) Sl 1, k1, [yo, k2tog] twice, yo 4 times, k2tog, yo, p2tog—13 sts.
Row 2 Yo, p2tog, k2, [p1, k1] 4 times, k1.
Row 3 Sl 1, [k1, yo, k2tog] twice, k4, yo, p2tog.
Row 4 Yo, p2tog, k5, [p1, k2] twice.
Row 5 Sl 1, k1, yo, k2tog, k2, yo, k2tog, k3, yo, p2tog.
Row 6 Yo, p2tog, k4, p1, k3, p1, k2.
Row 7 Sl 1, k1, yo, k2tog, k3, yo, k2tog, k2, yo, p2tog.
Row 8 Yo, p2tog, k3, p1, k4, p1, k2.
Row 9 Sl 1, k1, yo, k2tog, k4, yo, k2tog, k1, yo, p2tog.
Row 10 Yo, p2tog, k2, p1, k5, p1, k2.
Row 11 Sl 1, k1, yo, k2tog, k5, yo, k2tog, yo, p2tog.
Row 12 Bind off 3 sts knitwise, then sl the st from RH needle back to LH needle, yo, p2tog, k5, p1, k2—10 sts.
Rep rows 1–12.

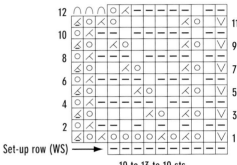

Set-up row (WS) →

10 to 13 to 10 sts

Stitch Key

☐ K on RS, p on WS

— K on WS

○ Yo

◹ K2tog on RS, p2tog on WS

◸ P2tog on RS

⌒ Bind off 1 st knitwise

▽ Sl 1 purlwise wyif

edgings

(begin on 9 sts)

Notes 1) On row 7, work triple yo as 3 separate sts.
2) Sts for St st portion were picked up after edging was knit.

Row 1 (RS) Yo, k2tog, yo, k1, yo, ssk, k4—10 sts.
Row 2 P5, k5.
Row 3 Yo, k2tog, yo, k3, yo, ssk, k3—11 sts.
Row 4 P4, k7.
Row 5 Yo, k2tog, yo, k2, ssk, k1, yo, ssk, k2.

Row 6 P3, k1, ssk, yo 3 times, k2tog, k3—12 sts.
Row 7 Yo, k2tog, yo, ssk, p1, k1, p1, k2tog, yo, k3.
Row 8 P4, k5, k2tog, k1—11 sts.
Row 9 Yo, k2tog, yo, ssk, k1, k2tog, yo, k4.
Row 10 P5, k3, k2tog, k1—10 sts.
Row 11 Yo, k2tog, yo, S2KP, yo, k5.
Row 12 P6, k1, k2tog, k1—9 sts.
Rep rows 1-12.

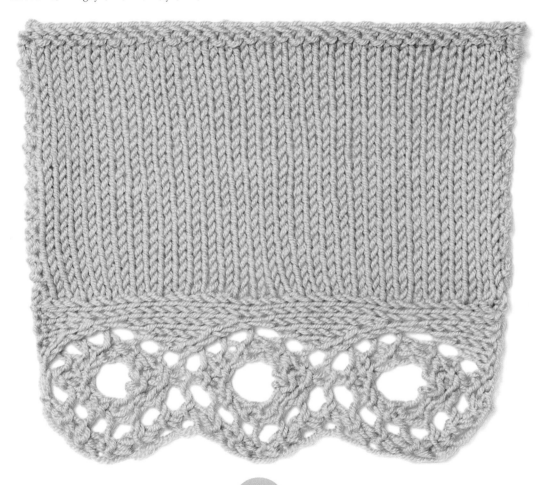

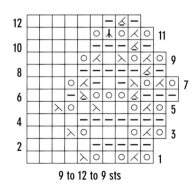

9 to 12 to 9 sts

Stitch Key

☐ K on RS, p on WS

⊟ P on RS, k on WS

⊙ Yo

⟋ K2tog on RS

⟍ Ssk on RS

⟋ K2tog on WS

⟍ Ssk on WS

⅄ S2KP

edgings

(begin on 23 sts)

Notes 1) Edging is knit onto an existing piece; sts are worked tog with live sts on needle. Number of sts on needle must be a multiple of 9 sts. 2) K2tog at end of every RS row joins one st of edging tog with one st from needle.

Row 1 (RS) Yo, k2, [yo, k2tog] 4 times, yo, k2, SK2P, yo twice, k2, k2tog, yo, k3, k2tog (last st of edging tog with one st from needle) — 25 sts.

Row 2 K2, k2tog, yo, k4, [p1, k1] into double yo, k12, k2tog, k1 tbl — 24 sts.

Row 3 Yo, k2, [yo, k2tog] 4 times, yo, k2, k2tog, k4, k2tog, yo, k3, k2tog — 25 sts.

Row 4 K2, k2tog, yo, k18, k2tog, k1 tbl — 24 sts.

Row 5 Yo, k2, [yo, k2tog] 4 times, yo, k1, SK2P, yo twice, k2tog, yo twice, k2, k2tog, yo, k3, k2tog — 27 sts.

Row 6 K2, k2tog, yo, k4, [p1, k1] into double yo, k1, [p1, k1] into double yo, k11, k2tog, k1 tbl — 26 sts.

Row 7 Yo, k2, [yo, k2tog] 4 times, yo, k10, k2tog, yo, k3, k2tog — 28 sts.

Row 8 K2, k2tog, yo, k21, k2tog, k1 tbl — 27 sts.

Row 9 Yo, k2, [yo, k2tog] 4 times, yo, k1, [SK2P, yo twice] twice, k2tog, yo twice, k2, k2tog, yo, k3, k2tog — 30 sts.

Row 10 K2, k2tog, yo, k4, [(p1, k1) into double yo, k1] twice, [p1, k1] into double yo, k11, k2tog, k1 tbl — 29 sts.

Row 11 Yo, k2, [yo, k2tog] 4 times, yo, k13, k2tog, yo, k3, k2tog — 31 sts.

Row 12 K2, k2tog, yo, k24, k2tog, k1 tbl — 30 sts.

Row 13 Yo, k2, [yo, k2tog] 4 times, yo, k1, [SK2P, yo twice] 3 times, k2tog, yo twice, k2, k2tog, yo, k3, k2tog — 33 sts.

Row 14 K2, k2tog, yo, k4, [(p1, k1) into double yo, k1] 3 times, [p1, k1] into double yo, k11, k2tog, k1 tbl — 32 sts.

Row 15 Yo, k2, [yo, k2tog] 4 times, yo, k16, k2tog, yo, k3, k2tog — 34 sts.

Row 16 K2, k2tog, yo, k27, k2tog, k1 tbl — 33 sts.

Row 17 Bind off 10 sts, k to last 6 sts of edging, k2tog, yo, k3, k2tog — 23 sts.

Row 18 K2, k2tog, yo, k19.

Rep rows 1-18.

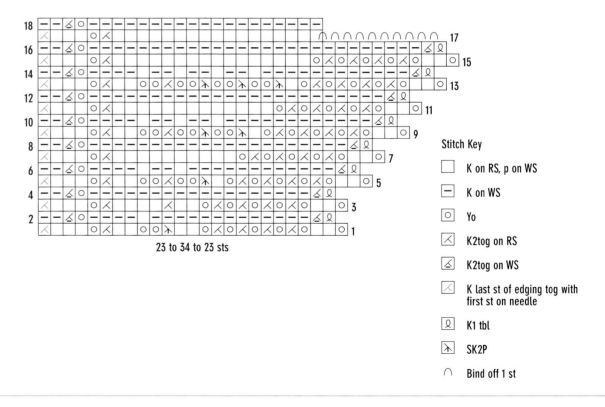

23 to 34 to 23 sts

Stitch Key

☐ K on RS, p on WS

– K on WS

○ Yo

╲ K2tog on RS

╱ K2tog on WS

⊠ K last st of edging tog with first st on needle

⊡ K1 tbl

⋌ SK2P

∩ Bind off 1 st

(begin on 30 sts)

Notes 1) Edging is knit onto an existing piece; sts are worked tog with live sts on needle. Number of sts on needle must be a multiple of 12 sts. 2) Sl sts at beg of WS rows purlwise wyif. 3) Ssk at end of every RS row joins one st of edging tog with one st from needle.

Row 1 (RS) Yo, k2tog, k1, yo, k3, yo, k2tog, k1, ssk, yo, k1, yo, ssk, k1, k2tog, yo, k1, yo, ssk, k1, k2tog, yo, k1, yo, k2tog, k1, ssk, yo, ssk (last st of edging tog with one st from needle) — 31 sts.

Row 2 and all WS rows Sl 1, p to last 2 sts, k2.

Row 3 Yo, k2tog, k1, yo, k4, yo, k2tog, k1, ssk, [(yo, k1) twice, SK2P, k1] twice, yo, k1, yo, k2tog, k1, ssk, yo, ssk — 32 sts.

Row 5 Yo, k2tog, k1, yo, k2, k2tog, yo, k1, yo, k2tog, k1, ssk, yo, k1, k2tog, yo, k1, yo, ssk, k1, k2tog, yo, k1, yo,

ssk, k1, yo, k2tog, k1, ssk, yo, ssk — 33 sts.

Row 7 Yo, k2tog, k1, yo, k2, k2tog, yo, k2, yo, k2tog, k1, ssk, yo, k2tog, [k1, yo] twice, k1, SK2P, [k1, yo] twice, k1, ssk, yo, k2tog, k1, ssk, yo, ssk — 34 sts.

Row 9 Yo, k2tog, k1, yo, k2, k2tog, yo, k3, yo, k2tog, k1, ssk, yo, k1, yo, ssk, k1, k2tog, yo, k1, yo, ssk, k1, k2tog, yo, k1, yo, k2tog, k1, ssk, yo, ssk — 35 sts.

Row 11 Yo, k2tog, k1, yo, k2, k2tog, yo, k4, yo, k2tog, k1, ssk, [(yo, k1) twice, SK2P, k1] twice, yo, k1, yo, k2tog, k1, ssk, yo, ssk — 36 sts.

Row 13 Yo, k2tog, ssk, [yo, ssk, k2] twice, yo, k2tog, k1, ssk, yo, k1, k2tog, yo, k1, yo, ssk, k1, k2tog, yo, k1, yo, ssk, k1, yo, k2tog, k1, ssk, yo, ssk — 35 sts.

Row 15 Yo, k2tog, ssk, yo, ssk, k2, yo, ssk, k1, yo, k2tog, k1, ssk, yo, k2tog, [k1, yo] twice, k1, SK2P, [k1, yo] twice, k1, ssk, yo, k2tog, k1, ssk, yo, ssk — 34 sts.

Row 17 Yo, k2tog, ssk, yo, ssk, k2, yo, ssk, yo, k2tog, k1, ssk, yo, k1, yo, ssk, k1, k2tog, yo, k1, yo, ssk, k1, k2tog, yo, k1, yo, k2tog, k1, ssk, yo, ssk — 33 sts.

Row 19 Yo, k2tog, ssk, yo, ssk, k3, yo, k2tog, k1, ssk, [(yo, k1) twice, SK2P, k1] twice, yo, k1, yo, k2tog, k1, ssk, yo, ssk — 32 sts.

Row 21 Yo, k2tog, ssk, yo, ssk, k2, yo, k2tog, k1, ssk, yo, k1, yo, ssk, k1, k2tog, yo, k1, yo, ssk, k1, yo, k2tog, k1, ssk, yo, ssk — 31 sts.

Row 23 Yo, k2tog, ssk, yo, ssk, k1, yo, k2tog, k1, ssk, yo, k2tog, [k1, yo] twice, k1, SK2P, [k1, yo] twice, k1, ssk, yo, k2tog, k1, ssk, yo, ssk — 30 sts.

Row 24 Rep row 2.

Rep rows 1-24.

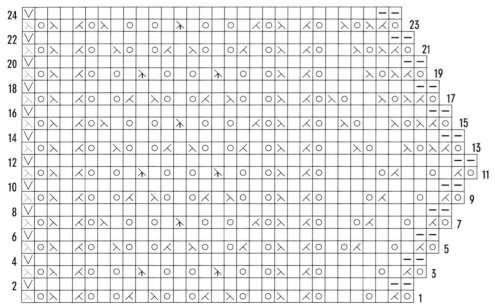

30 to 36 to 30 sts

Stitch Key

☐ K on RS, p on WS

▬ K on WS

◯ Yo

╱ K2tog

╲ Ssk

⋁ Sl 1 purlwise wyif

⊠ Ssk (last st of edging tog with one st from needle

⋔ SK2P

41

(multiple of 7 sts)
Rows 1–4 Knit.
Row 5 (RS) *K1, k2tog, yo, k1, yo, ssk, k1; rep from * to end.
Row 6 *Ssp, yo, p3, yo, p2tog; rep from * to end.

Row 7 *K1, yo, k2tog, yo, SK2P, yo, k1; rep from * to end.
Row 8 *P1, yo, p2tog, p1, ssp, yo, p1; rep from * to end.
Row 9 *K2, yo, SK2P, yo, k2; rep from * to end.
Rows 10–12 Knit.

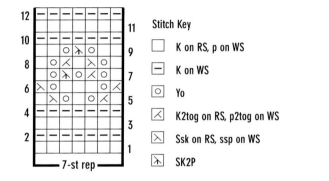

Stitch Key

☐	K on RS, p on WS
—	K on WS
⊙	Yo
⤡	K2tog on RS, p2tog on WS
⤢	Ssk on RS, ssp on WS
⤤	SK2P

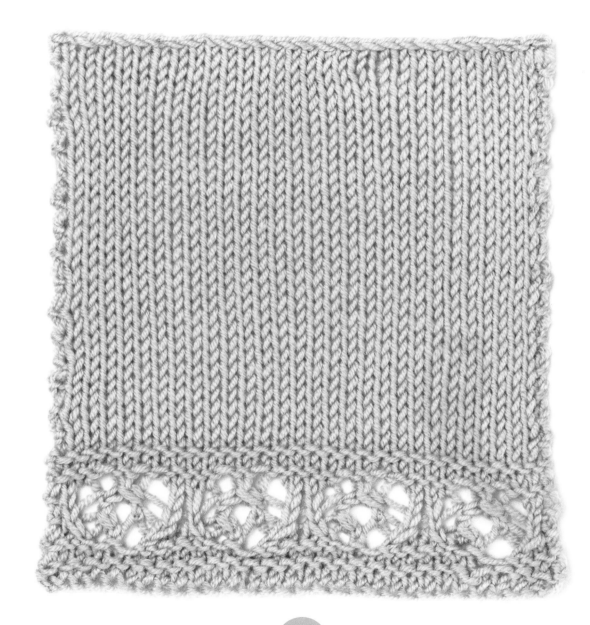

(begin on 10 sts)

Note Sts for St st portion were picked up after edging was knit.

Row 1 (RS) K1, k2tog, yo, k3, [yo, k2tog] twice.

Row 2 Yo, k1, yo, k2tog, yo, k7—12 sts.

Row 3 K1, k2tog, yo, k5, [yo, k2tog] twice.

Row 4 Yo, k1, yo, k2tog, yo, k9—14 sts.

Row 5 K1, k2tog, yo, k7, [yo, k2tog] twice.

Row 6 Yo, k1, yo, k2tog, yo, k11—16 sts.

Row 7 K1, k2tog, yo, k9, [yo, k2tog] twice.

Row 8 [Yo, k2tog] 3 times, k10.

Row 9 K1, k2tog, yo, k6, [k2tog, yo] twice, k3tog—14 sts.

Row 10 [Yo, k2tog] 3 times, k8.

Row 11 K1, k2tog, yo, k4, [k2tog, yo] twice, k3tog—12 sts.

Row 12 [Yo, k2tog] 3 times, k6.

Row 13 K1, k2tog, yo, k2, [k2tog, yo] twice, k3tog—10 sts.

Row 14 [Yo, k2tog] 3 times, k4.

Rep rows 1–14.

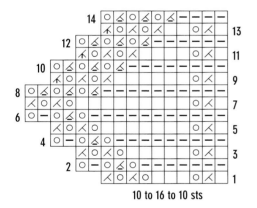

10 to 16 to 10 sts

Stitch Key

☐ K on RS

— K on WS

◉ Yo

◩ K2tog on RS

◩ K2tog on WS

⩓ K3tog

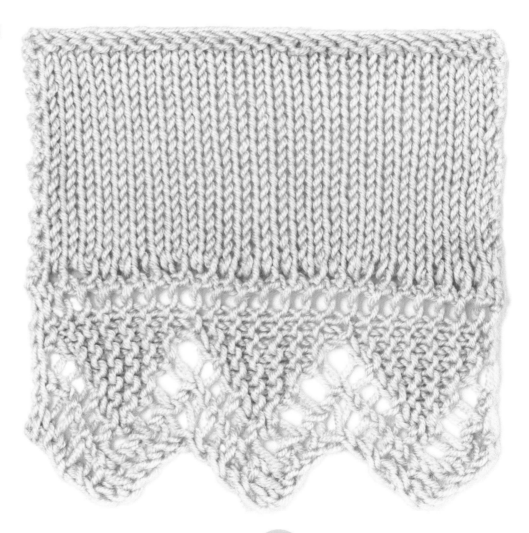

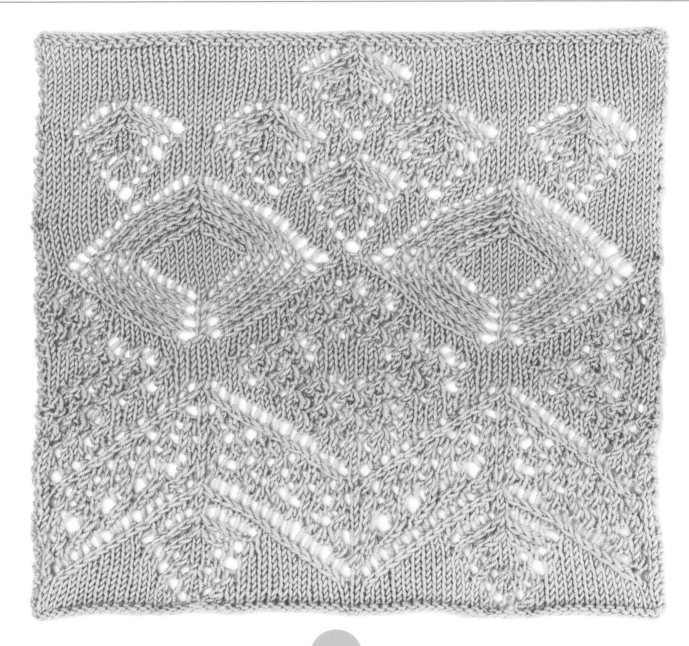

(multiple of 30 sts plus 1)

Row 1 (RS) K15, *yo, k2tog, k28; rep from *, end last rep k14 (instead of 28).

Rows 2 and 4 Purl.

Row 3 K13, *k2tog, yo, k1, yo, k2tog, k25; rep from *, end last rep k13 (instead of 25).

Row 5 K12, *k2tog, yo, k3, yo, k2tog, k23; rep from *, end last rep k12 (instead of 23).

Row 6 P1, *yo, p2tog, p25, ssp, yo, p1; rep from * to end.

Row 7 K1, *k1, yo, SKP, k8, yo, k2tog, yo, k3tog, yo, k2tog, yo, k8, k2tog, yo, k2; rep from * to end.

Row 8 P2tog, yo, *p1, yo, p2tog, p21, ssp, yo, p1, yo, p3tog, yo; rep from *, end last rep yo, p2tog (instead of yo, p3tog, yo).

Row 9 K1, *k2tog, yo, k1, yo, SKP, k4, [k2tog, yo, k1, yo, k2tog, k1] twice, k3, k2tog, yo, k1, yo, k2tog, k1; rep from * to end.

Row 10 P1, *yo, p2tog, p2, yo, p2tog, p17, ssp, yo, p2, p2tog, yo, p1; rep from * to end.

Row 11 K1, *k2, k2tog, yo, k1, yo, SKP, k2, [yo, SKP] twice, k3, [k2tog, yo] twice, k2, k2tog, yo, k1, yo, k2tog, k3; rep from * to end.

Row 12 P1, *p2, yo, p3tog, yo, p1, yo, p2tog, p2, [yo, p2tog] twice, p1, [ssp, yo] twice, p2, ssp, yo, p1, yo, p3tog, yo, p3; rep from * to end.

Row 13 K1, *k2tog, yo, k1, yo, k2tog, [k2, yo, SKP] twice, yo, k3tog, yo, [k2tog, yo, k2] twice, k2tog, yo, k1, yo, k2tog, k1; rep from * to end.

Row 14 P1, *p5, p2tog, yo, p1, yo, p2tog, p2, yo, p2tog, p1, ssp, yo, p2, ssp, yo, p1, yo, p2tog, p6; rep from * to end.

Row 15 K1, *[yo, k2tog] twice, k1, yo, k3tog, yo, k1, yo, SKP, k2, yo, k3tog, yo, k2, k2tog, yo, k1, yo, k3tog, yo, k1, [k2tog, yo] twice, k1; rep from * to end.

Row 16 P1, *p6, yo, p2tog, p2, yo, p2tog, p5, ssp, yo, p2, p2tog, yo, p7; rep from * to end.

Row 17 K1, *[k2tog, yo] 3 times, k2, k2tog, yo, k1, yo, SKP, k3, k2tog, yo, k1, yo, k2tog, k2, [yo, k2tog] 3 times, k1; rep from* to end.

Row 18 P1, *p8, yo, p3tog, yo, p1, yo, p2tog, p1, ssp, yo, p1, yo, p3tog, yo, p9; rep from * to end.

Row 19 K1, *yo, SKP, [yo, k2tog] 3 times, k1, yo, k2tog, k2, yo, k3tog, yo, k2, k2tog, yo, k1, [k2tog, yo] 4 times, k1; rep from * to end.

Row 20 P1, *p1, yo, p2tog, p8, p2tog, yo, p3, yo, p2tog, p8, ssp, yo, p2; rep from * to end.

Row 21 K1, *k2, yo, SKP, [k2tog, yo] 3 times, k1, [yo, k3tog, yo, k1] twice, [yo, k2tog] 3 times, k2tog, yo, k3; rep from * to end.

Row 22 P1, *p3, yo, p2tog, p7, yo, p2tog, p1, p2tog, yo, p7, ssp, yo, p4; rep from * to end.

Row 23 K2tog, yo, *k3, [yo, SKP] 4 times, k5, [k2tog, yo] 4 times, k3, yo, k3tog, yo; rep from *, end last rep yo, k2tog (instead of yo, k3tog, yo).

Row 24 K1, *yo, p2tog, p3, yo, p2tog, p15, ssp, yo, p3, p2tog, yo, k1; rep from * to end.

Row 25 K1, *k1, yo, k3tog, yo, k2, yo, SKP, [SKP, yo] 3 times, k1, [yo, k2tog] 3 times, k2tog, yo, k2, yo, k3tog, yo, k2; rep from * to end.

Row 26 P1, *p2tog, yo, k1, yo, p2tog, p2, yo, p2tog, p11, ssp, yo, p2, p2tog, yo, k1, yo, p2tog, p1; rep from * to end.

Row 27 K2tog, yo, *k3, yo, k2tog, k2, [yo, SKP] 3 times, k1, [k2tog, yo] 3 times, k2, k2tog, yo, k3, yo, k3tog, yo; rep from *, end last rep yo, k2tog (instead of yo, k3tog, yo).

Row 28 K1, *yo, p2tog, k1, p2tog, yo, p4, yo, p2tog, p7, ssp, yo, p4, yo, p2tog, k1, p2tog, yo, k1; rep from * to end.

Row 29 K1, *k1, yo, k3tog, yo, k6, yo, [SKP] twice, yo, k1, yo, [k2tog] twice, yo, k6, yo, k3tog, yo, k2; rep from * to end.

Row 30 K1, *p2tog, yo, k1, yo, p2tog, k1, p5, yo, p2tog, p3, ssp, yo, p5, k1, p2tog, yo, k1, yo, p2tog, k1; rep from * to end.

Row 31 K2tog, yo, *k3, yo, k3tog, yo, k5, yo, SKP, k1, k2tog, yo, k5, yo, k3tog, yo, k3, yo, k3tog, yo; rep from *, end last rep yo, k2tog (instead of yo, k3tog, yo).

Row 32 P1, *yo, p2tog, k1, p2tog, yo, k1, yo, p2tog, k1, p4, yo, p3tog, yo, p4, k1, p2tog, yo, k1, yo, p2tog, k1, p2tog, yo, p1; rep from * to end.

Row 33 K1, *k1, yo, k3tog, yo, k3, yo, k3tog, yo, k9, yo, k3tog, yo, k3, yo, k3tog, yo, k2; rep from * to end.

Row 34 P1, *p2, k1, yo, p2tog, k1, p2tog, yo, k1, yo, p2tog, p7, p2tog, yo, k1, yo, p2tog, k1, p2tog, yo, k1, p3; rep from * to end.

Row 35 K1, *k4, yo, k3tog, yo, k3, yo, k2tog, k5, k2tog, yo, k3, yo, k3tog, yo, k5; rep from * to end.

Row 36 P1, *p3, p2tog, yo, k1, yo, p2tog, k1, p2tog, yo, k1, p5, k1, yo, p2tog, k1, p2tog, yo, k1, yo, p2tog, p4; rep from * to end.

Row 37 K1, *k3, yo, k2tog, k2, yo, k3tog, yo, k9, yo, k3tog, yo, k2, k2tog, yo, k4; rep from * to end.

Row 38 Rep row 34.

Row 39 K1, *k4, yo, k3tog, yo, k15, yo, k3tog, yo, k5; rep from * to end.

Row 40 P1, *yo, p2tog, k1, p2tog, yo, k1, yo, p2tog, p5, yo, p3tog, yo, p5, p2tog, yo, k1, yo, p2tog, k1, p2tog, yo, p1; rep from * to end.

Row 41 K1, *k1, yo, k3tog, yo, k7, k2tog, yo, k3, yo, SKP, k7, yo, k3tog, yo, k2; rep from * to end.

Row 42 K1, *p2tog, yo, k1, yo, p2tog, k1, p4, [ssp, yo] twice, p1, [yo, p2tog] twice, p4, k1, p2tog, yo, k1, yo, p2tog, k1; rep from * to end.

Row 43 K2tog, yo, *k3, yo, k2tog, k3, [k2tog, yo] twice, k3, [yo, SKP] twice, k3, k2tog, yo, k3, yo, k3tog, yo; rep from *, end last rep yo, k2tog (instead of yo, k3tog, yo).

Row 44 K1, *yo, p2tog, k1, p2tog, yo, k1, p2, [ssp, yo] 3 times, p1, [yo, p2tog] 3 times, p2, k1, yo, p2tog, k1, p2tog, yo, k1; rep from * to end.

Row 45 K1, *k1, yo, k3tog, yo, k3, [k2tog, yo] 3 times, k3, [yo, SKP] 3 times, k3, yo, k3tog, yo, k2; rep from * to end.

Row 46 K1, *p2tog, yo, k1, yo, p2tog, p1, [ssp, yo] 4 times, p1, [yo, p2tog] 4 times, p1, p2tog, yo, k1, yo, p2tog, k1; rep from * to end.

Row 47 K2tog, yo, *k4, [k2tog, yo] 4 times, k3, [yo, SKP] 4 times, k4, yo, k3tog, yo; rep from *, end last rep yo, k2tog (instead of yo, k3tog, yo).

Row 48 K1, *yo, p2tog, p2, [ssp, yo] 4 times, p5, [yo, p2tog] 4 times, p2, p2tog, yo, k1; rep from * to end.

Row 49 K1, *k3, [k2tog, yo] 4 times, k7, [yo, SKP] 4 times, k4; rep from * to end.

Row 50 P1, *p2, [ssp, yo] 4 times, p9, [yo, p2tog] 4 times, p3; rep from * to end.

Row 51 K1, *k1, [k2tog, yo] 4 times, k11, [yo, SKP] 4 times, k2; rep from * to end.

Row 52 P1, *[ssp, yo] 4 times, p13, [yo, p2tog] 4 times, p1; rep from * to end.

Row 53 K1, *k2, [yo, k2tog] twice, [yo, SKP] twice, k9, [k2tog, yo] twice, [SKP, yo] twice, k3; rep from * to end.

Row 54 P1, *p3, yo, ssp, [yo, p2tog] 3 times, p7, [ssp, yo] 3 times, p2tog, yo, p2, p2tog, yo; rep from *, end last rep p4 (instead of p2, p2tog, yo).

Row 55 K1, *k4, [yo, SKP] 4 times, k5, [k2tog, yo] 4 times, k5; rep from * to end.

Row 56 P6, [yo, p2tog] 4 times, p2, *p1, [ssp, yo] 4 times, p3, p2tog, yo, p1, yo, p2tog, p3, [yo, p2tog] 4 times, p2; rep from * to last 15 sts, end p1, [ssp, yo] 4 times, p6.

Row 57 K1, *k6, [yo, SKP] 4 times, k1, [k2tog, yo] 4 times, k7; rep from * to end.

Row 58 P8, [yo, p2tog] 3 times, yo, p3tog, yo, *[ssp, yo] 3 times, p4, p2tog, yo, p3, yo, p2tog, p4, [yo, p2tog] 3 times, yo, p3tog, yo; rep from * to last 14 sts, end [ssp, yo] 3 times, p8.

Row 59 K1, *k8, [yo, SKP] 3 times, k1, [k2tog, yo] 3 times, k9; rep from * to end.

Row 60 P10, [yo, p2tog] twice, yo, p3tog, yo, *[ssp, yo] twice, p6, yo, p2tog, yo, p3tog, yo, p2tog, yo, p6, [yo, p2tog] twice, yo, p3tog, yo; rep from * to last 14 sts, end [ssp, yo] twice, p10.

Row 61 K1, *k10, [yo, SKP] twice, k1, [k2tog, yo] twice, k11; rep from * to end.

Row 62 P7, p2tog, yo, p3, yo, p2tog, yo, p3tog, yo, *ssp, yo, p2, p2tog, yo, p2, [p2tog, yo, p1, yo, p2tog, p1] twice, p2tog, yo, p3, yo, p2tog, yo, p3tog, yo; rep from * to last 14 sts, end ssp, yo, p2, p2tog, yo, p8.

Row 63 K13, *yo, SKP, k1, k2tog, yo, k25; rep from *, end last rep k13 (instead of 25).

Row 64 P6, p2tog, yo, p1, yo, p2tog, p3, yo, p3tog, yo, *p3, p2tog, yo, p1, [yo, p2tog] 3 times, p3, [ssp, yo] twice, p2tog, yo, p1, yo, p2tog, p3, yo, p3tog, yo; rep from * to last 14 sts, end p3, p2tog, yo, p1, yo, p2tog, p6.

Row 65 K26, *[yo, SKP] twice, k1, [k2tog, yo] twice, k21; rep from * to last 5 sts, end k5.

Row 66 P5, p2tog, yo, p3, yo, p2tog, p7, *p2tog, yo, p3, yo, p2tog, p1, yo, p2tog, yo, p3tog, yo, ssp, yo, p1, p2tog, yo, p3, yo, p2tog, p7; rep from * to last 12 sts, end p2tog, yo, p3, yo, p2tog, p5.

Row 67 K28, *yo, SKP, k1, k2tog, yo, k25; rep from * to last 3 sts, end k3.

Row 68 P5, yo, p2tog, yo, p3tog, yo, p2tog, yo, p7, *yo, p2tog, yo, p3tog, yo, p2tog, yo, p3, yo, p3tog, yo, p3, yo, p2tog, yo, p3tog, yo, p2tog, yo, p7; rep from * to last 12 sts, end yo, p2tog, yo, p3tog, yo, p2tog, yo, p5.

Rows 69 and 71 Knit.

Row 70 P1, *[p2, (p2tog, yo, p1, yo, p2tog, p1) twice, p2; rep from * to end.

Row 72 P3, [yo, p2tog] twice, p3, [ssp, yo] twice, p3, *[yo, p2tog] twice, p3, [ssp, yo] twice, p1, p2tog, yo, p2, [yo, p2tog] twice, p3, [ssp, yo] twice, p3; rep from * to last 14 sts, end [yo, p2tog] twice, p3, [ssp, yo] twice, p3.

Row 73 K1, *k3, [yo, SKP] twice, k1, [k2tog, yo] twice, k5, [yo, SKP] twice, k1, [k2tog, yo] twice, k4; rep from * to end.

Row 74 P5, yo, p2tog, yo, p3tog, yo, SKP, yo, p7, *yo, p2tog, yo, p3tog, yo, ssp, yo, p2, p2tog, yo, p1, yo, p2tog, p2, yo, p2tog, yo, p3tog, yo, ssp, yo, p7; rep from * to last 12 sts, end yo, p2tog, yo, p3tog, yo, ssp, yo, p5.

Row 75 K1, *k5, yo, SKP, k1, k2tog, yo, k9, yo, SKP, k1, k2tog, yo, k6; rep from * to end.

Row 76 P7, yo, p3tog, yo, p11, *yo, p3tog, yo, p3, p2tog, yo, p3, yo, p2tog, p3, yo, p3tog, yo, p11; rep from * to last 10 sts, end yo, p3tog, yo, p7.

Rows 77, 79 and 81 Knit.

Row 78 P27, *yo, p2tog, yo, p3tog, yo, p2tog, yo, p23; rep from * to last 4 sts, end p4.

Row 80 P25, *p2tog, yo, p1, yo, p2tog, p1, p2tog, yo, p1, yo, p2tog, p19; rep from * to last 6 sts, end p6.

Row 82 P25, *[yo, p2tog] twice, p3, [ssp, yo] twice, p19; rep from * to last 6 sts, end p6.

Row 83 K26, *[yo, SKP] twice, k1, [k2tog, yo] twice, k21; rep from * to last 5 sts, end k5.

Row 84 P27, *yo, p2tog, yo, p3tog, yo, ssp, yo, p23; rep from * to last 4 sts, end p4.

Row 85 K28, *yo, SKP, k1, k2tog, yo, k25; rep from * to last 3 sts, end k3.

Row 86 P29, *yo, p3tog, yo, p27; rep from * to last 2 sts, end p2.

Stitch Key

☐ K on RS, p on WS

⊟ P on RS, k on WS

⊙ Yo

⊠ K2tog on RS, p2tog on WS

⊠ SKP on RS, Ssp on WS

⊠ K3tog on RS, p3tog on WS

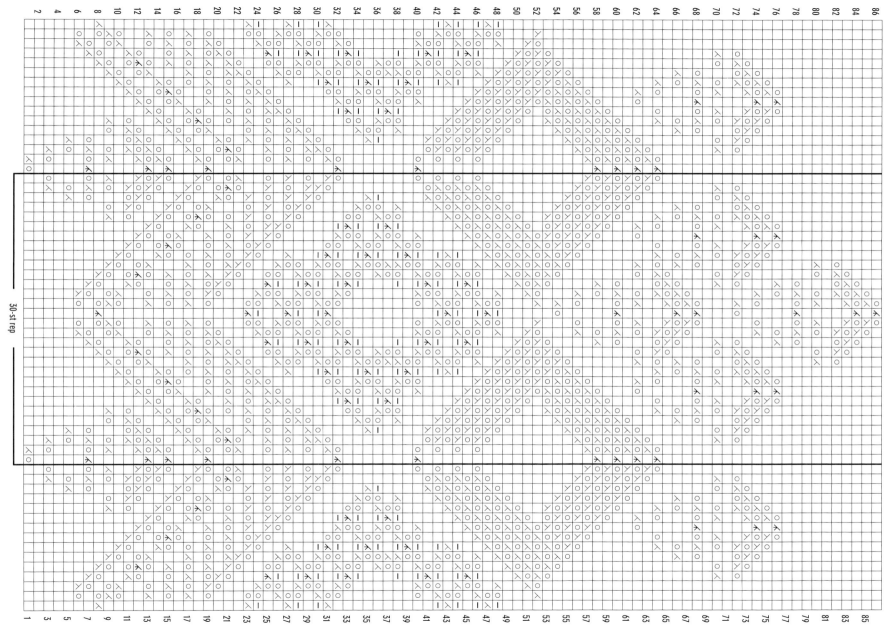

30-st rep

(multiple of 18 sts plus 1)

Rows 1, 3 and 5 (RS) Knit.

Rows 2 and 4 K1, *sl 2 sts purlwise wyib, k1; rep from * to end.

Row 6 P1, *yo, p4, p2tog, [k1, p1] twice, k1, ssp, p4, yo, p1; rep from * to end.

Row 7 *K2, yo, k4, ssk, p1, k1, p1, k2tog, k4, yo, k1; rep from *, end k1.

Row 8 P1, *p2, yo, p4, p2tog, k1, ssp, p4, yo, p3; rep from * to end.

Row 9 *K4, yo, k4, k3tog, k4, yo, k3; rep from *, end k1.

Rows 10, 12, and 14 Purl.

Rows 11 and 13 *P1, sl 2 sts purlwise wyif; rep from *, end p1.

Row 15 *K1, yo, k4, ssk, [p1, k1] twice, p1, k2tog, k4, yo; rep from *, end k1.

Row 16 P1, *p1, yo, p4, p2tog, k1, p1, k1, ssp, p4, yo, p2; rep from * to end.

Row 17 *K3, yo, k4, ssk, p1, k2tog, k4, yo, k2; rep from *, end k1.

Row 18 P1, *p3, yo, p4, p3tog, p4, yo, p4; rep from * to end.

Rep rows 1–18 once more.

Rows 19-22 Rep rows 1–4.

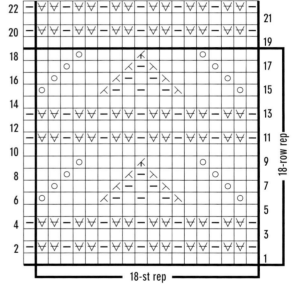

Stitch Key

☐ K on RS, p on WS

— P on RS, k on WS

☉ Yo

◿ K2tog on RS, p2tog on WS

◺ Ssk on RS, ssp on WS

↗ K3tog on RS, p3tog on WS

⊻ Sl 1 purlwise with yarn at RS of work

(multiple of 10 sts)

Row 1 (RS) K2, p1, k2, yo, ssk, *k8, yo, ssk; rep from * to last 13 sts, k10, p1, k2.

Row 2 P2, k1, p2, *yo, p2tog, p5, ssp, yo, p1; rep from * to last 5 sts, p2, k1, p2.

Row 3 K2, p1, k4, *yo, ssk, k3, k2tog, yo, k3; rep from * to last 3 sts, p1, k2.

Row 4 P2, k1, p4, *yo, p2tog, p1, ssp, yo, p5; rep from * to last 3 sts, k1, p2.

Row 5 K2, p1, k4, *k2, yo, SK2P, yo, k5; rep from * to last 3 sts, p1, k2.

Row 6 P2, k1, p5, *ssp, yo, p3; rep from * to last 7 sts, ssp, yo, p2, k1, p2.

Row 7 K2, p1, *k3, yo, ssk; rep from * to last 7 sts, k4, p1, k2.

Row 8 P2, k1, *p3, ssp, yo; rep from * to last 7 sts, p4, k1, p2.

Row 9 K2, p1, k2, *k3, yo, ssk; rep from * to last 5 sts, k2, p1, k2.

Row 10 P2, k1, p1, *ssp, yo, p3; rep from * to last 6 sts, p3, k1, p2.

Row 11 K2, p1, k2, *yo, ssk, k3; rep from * to last 5 sts, k2, p1, k2.

Rows 12–15 Rep rows 2–5.

Row 16 P2, k1, p3, *p3, yo, p2tog; rep from * to last 4 sts, p1, k1, p2.

Row 17 K2, p1, k2, *k3, k2tog, yo; rep from * to last 5 sts, k2, p1, k2.

Row 18 P2, k1, *p3, yo, p2tog; rep from * to last 7 sts, p4, k1, p2.

Row 19 K2, p1, *k3, k2tog, yo; rep from * to last 7 sts, k4, p1, k2.

Row 20 P2, k1, p5, *yo, p2tog, p3; rep from * to last 7 sts, yo, p2tog, p2, k1, p2.

Row 21 K2, p1, k1, *k2tog, yo, k3; rep from * to last 6 sts, k3, p1, k2.

Rows 22–25 Rep rows 2–5.

Row 26 P2, k1, p to last 3 sts, k1, p2.

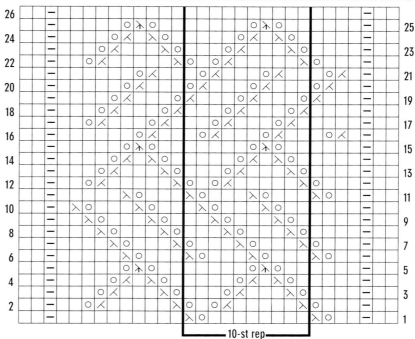

Stitch Key

☐ K on RS, p on WS

⊟ P on RS, k on WS

⊙ Yo

⟋ K2tog on RS, p2tog on WS

⟍ Ssk on RS, ssp on WS

⋏ SK2P

(begin on 8 sts)

Notes 1) On row 2, work triple yo from row 1 as 3 separate sts. 2) Sts for St st portion were picked up aafter edging was knit.

Row 1 (RS) Yo, p2tog, [k1, p1, k1, p1, k1] into a st, yo, p2tog, k1, yo 3 times, k2—15 sts.

Row 2 K3, p1, k2, yo, p2tog, k5, yo, p2tog.

Row 3 Yo, p2tog, k5, yo, p2tog, k6.

Row 4 K6, yo, p2tog, k5, yo, p2tog.

Row 5 Yo, p2tog, ssk, k1, k2tog, yo, p2tog, k6—13 sts.

Row 6 Bind off 3 sts, k2, yo, p2tog, SK2P, yo, p2tog—8 sts.

Rep rows 1–6.

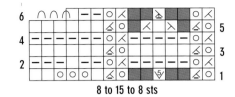

8 to 15 to 8 sts

Stitch Key

☐ K on RS, p on WS	◹ K2tog on RS, p2tog on WS	◺ SK2P on WS	▨ No stitch
▭ K on WS	◸ P2tog on RS	∩ Bind off 1 st	
⊙ Yo	◹ Ssk	⑤ [k1, p1, k1, p1, k1] into a st	

chevrons

55 feather and fan

(multiple of 24 sts)
Row 1 (RS) Knit.
Rows 2 and 4 Purl.
Row 3 *[K2tog] 4 times, [yo, k1] 8 times,
[k2tog] 4 times; rep from * to end.
Rep rows 1–4.

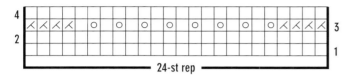

Stitch Key

⬜ K on RS, p on WS

⊙ Yo

⟋ K2tog

55

56 feather and fan II

(multiple of 24 sts)
Row 1 (RS) Knit.
Rows 2 and 4 Purl.
Row 3 *[P2tog] 4 times, [yo, k1] 8 times,
[p2tog] 4 times; rep from * to end.
Rep rows 1–4.

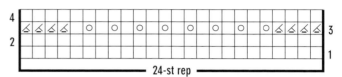

Stitch Key

⬜ K on RS, p on WS

⊙ Yo

◿ P2tog

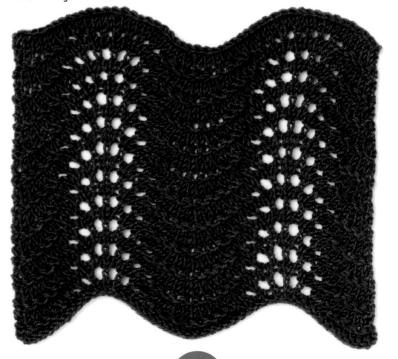

56

57 virginia reel

(multiple of 15 sts plus 1)
Row 1 (RS) K1, *k3tog, sl 1 knitwise, place slipped st and k3tog on LH needle, psso the k3tog, sl resulting st to RH needle, [yo, k1] 6 times, sl 1 knitwise, k3tog, psso, k1; rep from * to end.
Row 2 Purl.
Rep rows 1–2.

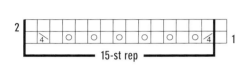

Stitch Key

	K on RS, p on WS
○	Yo
④	K3tog, sl 1 knitwise, place slipped st and k3tog back on LH needle, psso, sl st back to RH needle
④	Sl 1 knitwise, k3tog, psso

58 simple chevron

(multiple of 10 sts plus 1)
Row 1 (RS) K1, *k4, yo, ssk, k4; rep from * to end.
Row 2 and all WS rows Purl.
Row 3 K1, *k2, k2tog, yo, k1, yo, ssk, k3; rep from * to end.
Row 5 K1, *k1, k2tog, yo, k3, yo, ssk, k2; rep from * to end.
Row 7 K1, *k2tog, yo, k5, yo, ssk, k1; rep from * to end.
Row 9 K2tog, *yo, k7, yo, SK2P; rep from *, end last rep ssk (instead of SK2P).
Row 10 Purl.
Rep rows 1–10.

Stitch Key

	K on RS, p on WS
○	Yo
╱	K2tog
╲	Ssk
⋏	SK2P

chevrons

(multiple of 13 sts)

(Note On WS rows, drop the extra yo when working a st above a double yo.)

Row 1 (RS) *P4, k2tog, yo twice, k1, yo twice, ssk, p4; rep from * to end.

Row 2 *K4, [p1, k1] twice, p1, k4;rep from * to end.

Row 3 *P3, k2tog, yo twice, p1, k1, p1, yo twice, ssk, p3; rep from * to end.

Row 4 *K3, [p1, k2] twice, p1, k3; rep from * to end.

Row 5 *P2, k2tog, yo twice, p2, k1, p2, yo twice, ssk, p2; rep from * to end.

Row 6 *K2, [p1, k3] twice, p1, k2; rep from * to end.

Row 7 *P1, k2tog, yo twice, p3, k1, p3, yo twice, ssk, p1; rep from * to end.

Row 8 *K1, [p1, k4] twice, p1, k1; rep from * to end.

Row 9 *K2tog, yo twice, p3, k3, p3, yo twice, ssk; rep from * to end.

Row 10 *P1, k4, p3, k4, p1; rep from * to end.

Rep rows 1–10.

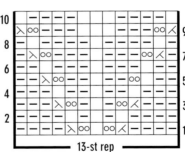

13-st rep

Stitch Key

☐ K on RS, p on WS

— P on RS, k on WS

oo Yo twice (on WS rows, drop the extra yo)

⟋ K2tog

⟍ Ssk

chevrons

(multiple of 44 sts plus 1)

Row 1 (WS) *P2, k1, p1, k1, p2, [k1, p1] twice, k1, p2, [k1, p1] 3 times, k1, p3, [k1, p1] 3 times, k1, p2, [k1, p1] twice, k1, p2, [k1, p1] twice; rep from *, end p1.

Row 2 K1, *k1, yo, [p1, k1, p1, ssk, yo twice, ssk] twice, [p1, k1] twice, k2tog, k1, ssk, [k1, p1] twice, [k2tog, yo twice, k2tog, p1, k1, p1] twice, yo, k2; rep from * to end.

Row 3 *P3, k1, p1, k1, p2, [k1, p1] twice, k1, p2, [k1, p1] twice, k1, p5, [(k1, p1) twice, k1, p2] twice, k1, p1, k1, p2; rep from *, end p1.

Row 4 K1, *k1, yo, [k1, p1] twice, [ssk, yo twice, ssk, p1, k1, p1] twice, k2tog, k1, ssk, [p1, k1, p1, k2tog, yo twice, k2tog] twice, [p1, k1] twice, yo, k2; rep from * to end.

Row 5 P2, *[(k1, p1) twice, k1, p2] twice, [k1, p1] twice, k1, p3, [(k1, p1) twice, k1, p2] twice, [k1, p1] 3 times; rep from *, end p1.

Row 6 K1, *k1, yo, [p1, k1] twice, [p1, ssk, yo twice, ssk, p1, k1] twice, k2tog, k1, ssk, [k1, p1, k2tog, yo twice, k2tog, p1] twice, [k1, p1] twice, yo, k2; rep from * to end.

Row 7 *P3, [(k1, p1) twice, k1, p2] twice, k1, p1, k1, p5, k1, p1, k1, p2, [(k1, p1) twice, k1, p2] twice; rep from *, end p1.

Row 8 K1, *k1, yo, [k1, p1] 3 times, ssk, yo twice, ssk, p1, k1, p1, ssk, yo twice, ssk, p1, k2tog, k1, ssk, p1, k2tog, yo twice, k2tog, p1, k1, p1, k2tog, yo twice, k2tog, [p1, k1] 3 times, yo, k2; rep from * to end.

Row 9 *P2, [k1, p1] 3 times, k1, p2, [k1, p1] twice, k1, p2, k1, p1, k1, p3, k1, p1, k1, p2, [k1, p1] twice, k1, p2, [k1, p1] 4 times; rep from *, end p1.

Row 10 K1, *k1, yo, [ssk, yo twice, ssk, p1, k1, p1] twice, ssk, yo twice, ssk, k2tog, k1, ssk, [k2tog, yo twice, k2tog, p1, k1, p1] twice, k2tog, yo twice, k2tog, yo, k2; rep from * to end.

Row 11 *P2, k1, p2, [(k1, p1) twice, k1, p2] twice, k1, p5, k1, p2, [(k1, p1) twice, k1, p2] twice, k1, p1; rep from *, end p1.

Row 12 K1, *k1, yo, p1, ssk, yo twice, ssk, p1, k1, p1, ssk, yo twice, ssk, [p1, k1] 3 times, k2tog, k1, ssk, [k1, p1] 3 times, k2tog, yo twice, k2tog, p1, k1, p1, k2tog, yo twice, k2tog, p1, yo, k2; rep from * to end.

Row 13 *P3, k1, p2, [k1, p1] twice, k1, p2, [k1, p1] 3 times, k1, p5, [k1, p1] 3 times, k1, p2, [k1, p1] twice, [k1, p2] twice; rep from *, end p1.

Row 14 K1, *k1, yo, [k1, p1, ssk, yo twice, ssk, p1] twice, [k1, p1] twice, k2tog, k1, ssk, [p1, k1] twice, [p1, k2tog, yo twice, k2tog, p1, k1] twice, yo, k2; rep from * to end.

Rep rows 1–14.

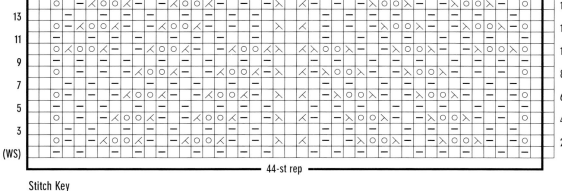

Stitch Key

☐ K on RS, p on WS	◹ K2tog
⊟ P on RS, k on WS	◿ Ssk
⊙ Yo	

61 christmas market

(multiple of 14 sts plus 1)
Row 1 (RS) K6, *k2tog, yo, k5; rep from *, end k2.
Row 2 and all WS rows Purl.
Row 3 K1, *yo, ssk, k2, k2tog, yo, k1; rep from * to end.
Row 5 K1, *k1, yo, ssk, k3, yo, ssk, k2, k2tog, yo, k2; rep from * to end.

Row 7 K1, *k2, yo, ssk, k5, k2tog, yo, k3; rep from * to end.
Row 9 K1, *k1, [yo, ssk] twice, k3, [k2tog, yo] twice, k2; rep from * to end.
Row 11 Rep row 7.
Row 13 K1, *k3, yo, ssk, k3, k2tog, yo, k4; rep from * to end.

Row 15 K5, *yo, ssk, k1, k2tog, yo, k3, k2tog, yo, k4; rep from * to last 10 sts, end yo, ssk, k1, k2tog, yo, k5.
Row 17 K1, *yo, ssk, k3, yo, SK2P, yo, k3, k2tog, yo, k1; rep from * to end.
Row 19 K7, *yo, ssk, k5; rep from *, end k1.
Row 20 Purl.

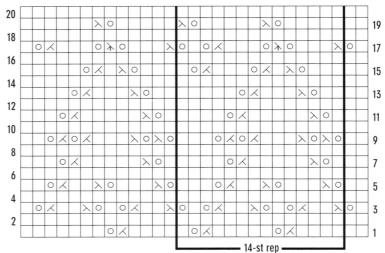

14-st rep

Stitch Key

☐ K on RS, p on WS

⊡ Yo

⟋ K2tog

⟍ Ssk

⅄ SK2P

62 broken chevron

(multiple of 22 sts)
Row 1 (RS) *K5, yo, ssk, k8, k2tog, yo, k5; rep from * to end.
Row 2 and all WS rows Purl.
Row 3 *K6, yo, ssk, k6, k2tog, yo, k6; rep from * to end.
Row 5 *K7, yo, ssk, k4, k2tog, yo, k7; rep from * to end.

Row 7 *K8, yo, ssk, k2, k2tog, yo, k8; rep from * to end.
Row 9 *K9, yo, ssk, k2tog, yo, k9; rep from * to end.
Row 11 *K4, k2tog, yo, k10, yo, ssk, k4; rep from * to end.
Row 13 *K3, k2tog, yo, k12, yo, ssk, k3; rep from * to end.
Row 15 *K2, k2tog, yo, k14, yo, ssk, k2; rep from * to end.

Row 17 *K1, k2tog, yo, k16, yo, ssk, k1;
rep from * to end.
Row 19 *K2tog, yo, k18, yo, ssk; rep from * to end.
Row 20 Purl.
Rep rows 1–20.

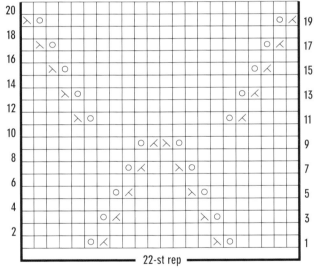

Stitch Key

☐ K on RS, p on WS

⊙ Yo

⊘ K2tog

⊠ Ssk

63 pigtails

(worked over 17 sts)
Row 1 (RS) K4, k2tog, k2, yo, p1, yo, k2, ssk, k4.
Row 2 and all WS rows P8, k1, p8.
Row 3 K3, k2tog, k2, yo, k1, p1, k1, yo, k2, ssk, k3.
Row 5 K2, k2tog, k2, yo, k2, p1, k2, yo, k2, ssk, k2.

Row 7 K1, k2tog, k2, yo, k3, p1, k3, yo, k2, ssk, k1.
Row 9 K2tog, k2, yo, k4, p1, k4, yo, k2, ssk.
Row 10 Rep row 2.
Rep rows 1–10.

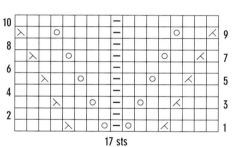

17 sts

Stitch Key

☐ K on RS, p on WS

— P on RS, k on WS

◎ Yo

⟋ K2tog

⟍ Ssk

64 double chevron

(multiple of 12 sts plus 1)
Row 1 (RS) *K1, yo, ssk, k7, k2tog, yo; rep from *, end k1.
Row 2 and all WS rows Purl.
Row 3 *K2, yo, ssk, k5, k2tog, yo, k1; rep from *, end k1.

Row 5 *K1, [yo, ssk] twice, k3, [k2tog, yo] twice; rep from *, end k1.
Row 7 *K2, [yo, ssk] twice, k1, [k2tog, yo] twice, k1; rep from *, end k1.

Row 9 *K3, yo, ssk, yo, S2KP, yo, k2tog, yo, k2; rep from *, end k1.
Row 11 *K4, yo, ssk, k1, k2tog, yo, k3; rep from *, end k1.
Row 13 *K5, yo, S2KP, yo, k4; rep from *, end k1.
Row 14 Purl.
Rep rows 1–14.

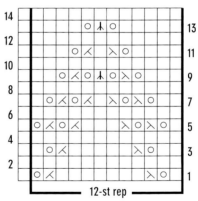

12-st rep

Stitch Key

☐ K on RS, p on WS

⊙ Yo

╱ K2tog

╲ Ssk

⅄ S2KP

65 sail away, ladies

Note This pattern can be knit in various multiples. The swatch shown here is a 16-stitch multiple.

(multiple of 10 sts plus 1)
Row 1 (RS) *K1, yo, k3, S2KP, k3, yo; rep from *, end k1.
Rows 2, 4 and 6 Purl.
Row 3 *K2, yo, k2, S2KP, k2, yo, k1; rep from *, end k1.
Row 5 *K3, yo, k1, S2KP, k1, yo, k2; rep from *, end k1.
Row 7 *K4, yo, S2KP, yo, k3; rep from *, end k1.
Row 8 Knit.
Row 9 *K2tog, yo; rep from *, end k1.
Row 10 Knit.
Rep rows 1–10.

(multiple of 14 sts plus 1)
Row 1 (RS) *K1, yo, k5, S2KP, k5, yo; rep from *, end k1.
Rows 2, 4, 6, 8 and 10 Purl.
Row 3 *K2, yo, k4, S2KP, k4, yo, k1; rep from *, end k1.
Row 5 *K3, yo, k3, S2KP, k3, yo, k2; rep from *, end k1.
Row 7 *K4, yo, k2, S2KP, k2, yo, k3; rep from *, end k1.
Row 9 *K5, yo, k1, S2KP, k1, yo, k4; rep from *, end k1.
Row 11 *K6, yo, S2KP, yo, k5; rep from *, end k1.
Row 12 Knit.
Row 13 *K2tog, yo; rep from *, end k1.
Row 14 Knit.
Rep rows 1–14.

(multiple of 16 sts plus 1)
Row 1 (RS) *K1, yo, k6, S2KP, k6, yo; rep from *, end k1.
Rows 2, 4, 6, 8, 10 and 12 Purl.
Row 3 *K2, yo, k5, S2KP, k5, yo, k1; rep from *, end k1.
Row 5 *K3, yo, k4, S2KP, k4, yo, k2; rep from *, end k1.
Row 7 *K4, yo, k3, S2KP, k3, yo, k3; rep from *, end k1.
Row 9 *K5, yo, k2, S2KP, k2, yo, k4; rep from *, end k1.
Row 11 *K6, yo, k1, S2KP, k1, yo, k5; rep from *, end k1.
Row 13 *K7, yo, S2KP, yo, k6; rep from *, end k1.
Row 14 Knit.
Row 15 *K2tog, yo; rep from *, end k1.
Row 16 Knit.
Rep rows 1–16.

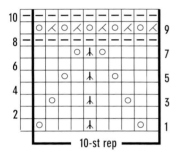

10-st rep

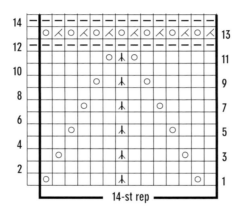

14-st rep

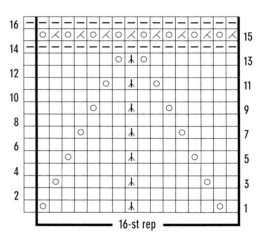

16-st rep

Stitch Key

☐	K on RS, p on WS
−	K on WS
⊙	Yo
╱	K2tog
⋏	S2KP

(multiple of 22 sts plus 1)
Row 1 (RS) *K1, yo, k9, S2KP, k9, yo; rep from *, end k1.
Rows 2, 4, 6, 8, 10, 12, 14, 16 and 18 Purl.
Row 3 *K2, yo, k8, S2KP, k8, yo, k1; rep from *, end k1.
Row 5 *K3, yo, k7, S2KP, k7, yo, k2; rep from *, end k1.
Row 7 *K4, yo, k6, S2KP, k6, yo, k3; rep from *, end k1.
Row 9 *K5, yo, k5, S2KP, k5, yo, k4; rep from *, end k1.
Row 11 *K6, yo, k4, S2KP, k4, yo, k5; rep from *, end k1.
Row 13 *K7, yo, k3, S2KP, k3, yo, k6; rep from *, end k1.
Row 15 *K8, yo, k2, S2KP, k2, yo, k7; rep from *, end k1.
Row 17 *K9, yo, k1, S2KP, k1, yo, k8; rep from *, end k1.
Row 19 *K10, yo, S2KP, yo, k9; rep from *, end k1.
Row 20 Knit.
Row 21 *K2tog, yo; rep from *, end k1.
Row 22 Knit.
Rep rows 1–22.

chevrons

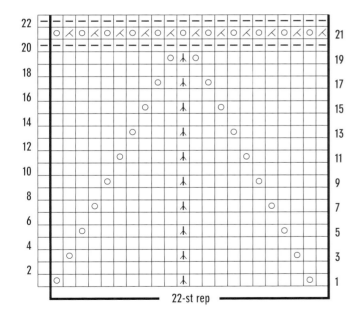

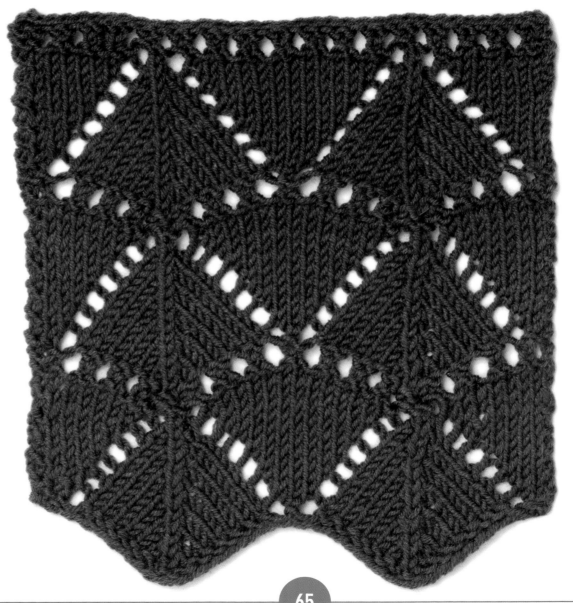

66 snowcapped

(multiple of 8 sts plus 5)

Row 1 (RS) K1, *k1, yo, ssk, k5; rep from * to last 4 sts, end k1, yo, ssk, k1.

Row 2 and all WS rows Purl.

Row 3 K2tog, *yo, k1, yo, ssk, k3, k2tog; rep from * to last 3 sts, end yo, k1, yo, ssk.

Row 5 K1, *k1, [yo, ssk] twice, k1, k2tog, yo; rep from * to last 4 sts, end k2tog, yo, k2.

Row 7 K2tog, *yo, k1, yo, ssk, yo, SK2P, yo, k2tog; rep from * to last 3 sts, end yo, k1, yo, ssk.

Row 9 K1, *k3, yo, ssk, yo, SK2P, yo; rep from *, end k4.

Row 11 K1, *k4, yo, SK2P, yo, k1; rep from *, end k4.

Row 13 K1, *k1, yo, ssk, k2, yo, ssk, k1; rep from * to last 4 sts, end k1, yo, ssk, k1.

Row 15 K1, *[yo, ssk] twice, k4; rep from * to last 4 sts, end [yo, ssk] twice.

Row 17 Rep row 1.

Row 19 K1, *k5, yo, ssk, k1; rep from *, end k4.

Row 21 K1, *k4, [yo, ssk] twice; rep from *, end k4.

Row 23 Rep row 13.

Rows 25–33 Rep rows 3–11.

Row 35 Rep row 19.

Row 36 Purl.

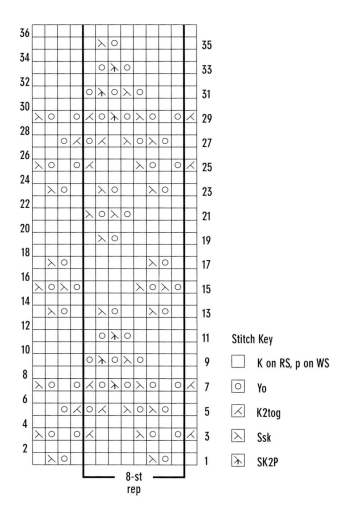

Stitch Key

☐	K on RS, p on WS
○	Yo
╱	K2tog
╲	Ssk
⋏	SK2P

8-st rep

67 crystal chandelier

(multiple of 8 sts plus 1)
Row 1 (RS) K1, *k1, k2tog, yo, k1, yo, ssk, k2; rep from * to end.
Row 2 and all WS rows Purl.
Row 3 K1, *k2tog, yo, k3, yo, ssk, k1; rep from * to end.
Row 5 [K2tog, yo] twice, *k1, yo, ssk, yo, S2KP, yo, k2tog, yo; rep from * to last 5 sts, end k1, [yo, ssk] twice.
Row 7 K1, *k2tog, yo, k3, yo, ssk, k1; rep from * to end.

Row 9 K2tog, yo, *k5, yo, S2KP, yo; rep from * to last 7 sts, end k5, yo, ssk.
Rows 11–19 Rep rows 1–9.
Rows 21, 23 and 25 K1, *yo, k1, ssk, k1, k2tog, k1, yo, k1; rep from * to end.
Row 26 Purl.
Rep rows 1–26.

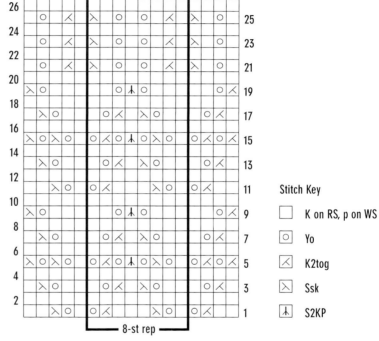

Stitch Key

	K on RS, p on WS
○	Yo
╱	K2tog
╲	Ssk
人	S2KP

68 teepees

(multiple of 14 sts plus 1)

Row 1 (RS) K1, *yo, ssk, yo, k3, S2KP, k3, yo, k2tog, yo, k1; rep from * to end.

Row 2 and all WS rows Purl.

Row 3 K1, *k1, yo, ssk, yo, k2, S2KP, k2, yo, k2tog, yo, k2; rep from * to end.

Row 5 K1, *k2, yo, ssk, yo, k1, S2KP, k1, yo, k2tog, yo, k3; rep from * to end.

Row 7 K1, *k3, yo, ssk, yo, S2KP, yo, k2tog, yo, k4; rep from * to end.

Row 9 K1, *k4, yo, k1, S2KP, k1, yo, k5; rep from * to end.

Row 11 K1, *k5, yo, S2KP, yo, k6; rep from * to end.

Row 12 Purl.

Rep rows 1–12.

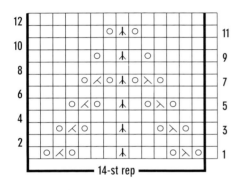

Stitch Key

☐ K on RS, p on WS

○ Yo

╱ K2tog

╲ Ssk

⅄ S2KP

69 pretty plumage

(multiple of 10 sts plus 1)

Row 1 (RS) K1, *yo, ssk, k2tog, yo, k1; rep from * to end.

Row 2 and all WS rows Purl.

Row 3 K1, *k1, yo, ssk, k3, k2tog, yo, k2; rep from * to end.

Row 5 K1, *k2, yo, ssk, k1, k2tog, yo, k3; rep from * to end.

Row 7 K1, *k3, yo, SK2P, yo, k4; rep from * to end.

Rows 9, 11 and 13 K1, *ssk, k2, yo, k1, yo, k2, k2tog, k1; rep from * to end.

Row 14 Purl.

Rep rows 1–14.

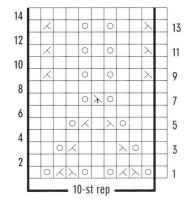

Stitch Key

☐	K on RS, p on WS
⊙	Yo
◿	K2tog
◺	Ssk
⋏	SK2P

70 manta rays

(multiple of 14 sts plus 3)
Row 1 (RS) K1, k2tog, *k5, yo, k1, yo, k5, S2KP; rep from *, end last rep ssk, k1 (instead of S2KP).
Row 2 and all WS rows Purl.
Row 3 K1, k2tog, *k4, yo, k3, yo, k4, S2KP; rep from *, end last rep ssk, k1 (instead of S2KP).

Row 5 K1, k2tog, *k3, yo, k5, yo, k3, S2KP; rep from *, end last rep ssk, k1 (instead of S2KP).
Row 7 K1, k2tog, *k2, yo, k1, k2tog, yo, k1, yo, ssk, k1, yo, k2, S2KP; rep from *, end last rep ssk, k1 (instead of S2KP).

Row 9 K1, k2tog, *k1, yo, k9, yo, k1, S2KP; rep from *, end last rep ssk, k1 (instead of S2KP).
Row 11 K1, k2tog, *yo, k1, [k2tog, yo] twice, k1, [yo, ssk] twice, k1, yo, S2KP; rep from *, end last rep ssk, k1 (instead of S2KP).
Row 12 Purl.
Rep rows 1–12.

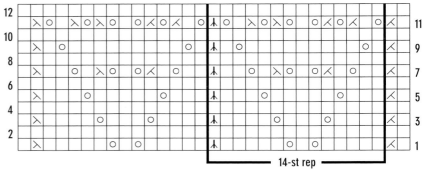

14-st rep

Stitch Key

☐	K on RS, p on WS
○	Yo
╱	K2tog
╲	Ssk
⅄	S2KP

allover

71 eyelet ridges

(multiple of 6 sts plus 3)
Row 1 (RS) P3, *yo, k3tog tbl, yo, p3; rep from * to end.
Row 2 *K3, p3; rep from *, end k3. .
Rep rows 1–2.

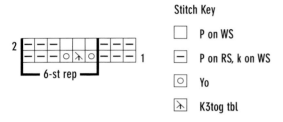

2 — — — — — | | | — — —
1 — — — o ⋏ o — — —
6-st rep

Stitch Key

☐ P on WS

— P on RS, k on WS

⊙ Yo

⋏ K3tog tbl

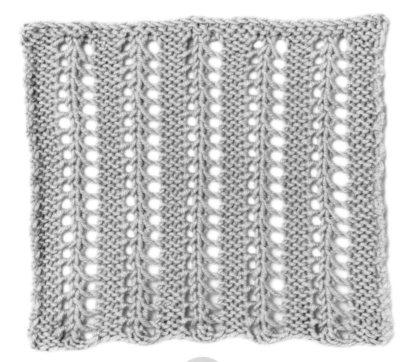

71

72 hanging vines

(multiple of 7 sts)
Row 1 (RS) *K2, k2tog, yo, k3; rep from * to end.
Row 2 and all WS rows Purl.
Row 3 *K1, k2tog, yo, k4; rep from * to end.
Row 5 Knit.

Row 7 *K3, yo, SKP, k2; rep from * to end.
Row 9 *K4, yo, SKP, k1; rep from * to end.
Row 11 Knit.
Row 12 Purl
Rep rows 1–12.

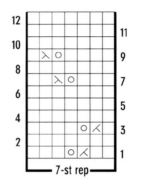

Stitch Key

☐ K on RS, p on WS

⊙ Yo

╱ K2tog

╲ SKP

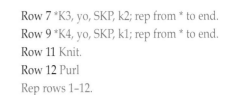

72

(multiple of 14 sts plus 1)

Row 1 (RS) [P1, k1] twice, p1, *k1, k2tog, yo, k2, p1, k1, p1, k3, p1, k1, p1; rep from * to last 10 sts, k1, k2tog, yo, k2, [p1, k1] twice, p1.

Row 2 and all WS rows [K1, p1] twice, k1, p5, *k1, p1, k1, ssp, yo, [p1, k1] twice, p5; rep from * to last 5 sts, [k1, p1] twice, k1.

Row 3 [P1, k1] twice, p1, *k2tog, yo, k1, yo, ssk, p1, k1, p1, k3, p1, k1, p1; rep from * to last 10 sts, k2tog, yo, k1, yo, ssk, [p1, k1] twice, p1.

Rows 5 and 7 [P1, k1] twice, p1, *k5, p1, k1, p1, k3, p1, k1, p1; rep from * to last 10 sts, k5, [p1, k1] twice, p1.

Row 8 Rep row 2.

Rep rows 1–8.

allover

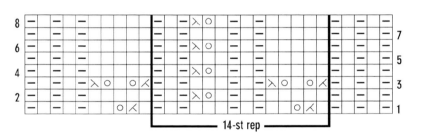

14-st rep

Stitch Key

☐ K on RS, p on WS

▬ P on RS, k on WS

○ Yo

◹ K2tog

◸ Ssk on RS, ssp on WS

(multiple of 8 sts plus 5)

Row 1 (RS) K1, *k1, yo, ssk, k5; rep from * to last 4 sts, end k1, yo, ssk, k1.

Row 2 and all WS rows Purl.

Row 3 K1, *[yo, ssk] twice, k4; rep from * to last 4 sts, end [yo, ssk] twice.

Row 5 Rep row 1.

Row 7 Knit.

Row 9 K1, *k5, yo, ssk, k1; rep from * to last 4 sts, end k4.

Row 11 K1, *k4, [yo, ssk] twice; rep from * to last 4 sts, end k4.

Row 13 Rep row 9.

Row 15 Knit.

Row 16 Purl.

Rep rows 1–16.

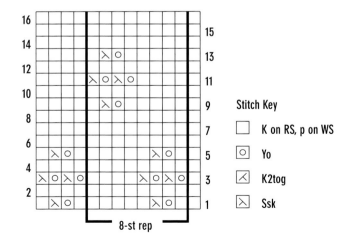

Stitch Key

☐ K on RS, p on WS

⊙ Yo

╱ K2tog

╲ Ssk

8-st rep

74

75 sweet violets

(multiple of 7 sts plus 3)
Row 1 (RS) K3, *k2tog, yo, k5; rep from * to end.
Row 2 and all WS rows Purl.
Row 3 K2, *k2tog, yo, k1, yo, ssk, k2; rep from *, end k1.
Row 5 Rep row 1.
Row 7 K2tog, yo, *k5, k2tog, yo; rep from *, end k1.
Row 9 K2, *yo, ssk, k2, k2tog, yo, k1; rep from *, end k1.
Row 11 Rep row 7.
Row 12 Purl.
Rep rows 1–12.

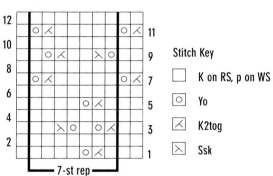

Stitch Key

☐	K on RS, p on WS
⊡	Yo
⟋	K2tog
⟍	Ssk

7-st rep

75

76 field of daisies

(multiple of 16 sts plus 1)
Row 1 (RS) K1, *k2, yo, SK2P, yo, k11; rep from * to end.
Row 2 Purl.
Row 3 K1, *k2tog, yo, p3, yo, ssk, k9; rep from * to end.
Row 4 *P10, k5, p1; rep from *, end p1.
Row 5 Rep row 1.
Rows 6 and 8 Purl.
Row 7 Knit.
Row 9 K1, *k10, yo, SK2P, yo, k3; rep from * to end.
Row 10 Purl.
Row 11 K1, *k8, k2tog, yo, p3, yo, ssk, k1; rep from * to end.
Row 12 *P2, k5, p9; rep from *, end p1.
Row 13 Rep row 9.
Rows 14 and 16 Purl.
Row 15 Knit.
Rep rows 1–16.

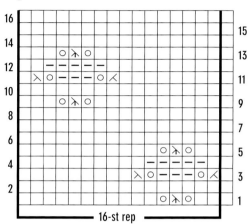

16-st rep

Stitch Key

☐	K on RS, p on WS
—	P on RS, k on WS
⊡	Yo
⟋	K2tog
⟍	Ssk
⅄	SK2P

76

(multiple of 20 sts plus 14)

Rows 1, 5 and 9 (RS) K5, *k2tog, yo twice, ssk, k16; rep from *, end last rep k5 (instead of 16).

Row 2 and all WS rows Purl (working [p1, k1] into double yos).

Rows 3 and 7 K3, *[k2tog, yo twice, ssk] twice, k12; rep from *, end last rep k3 (instead of 12).

Row 11 Knit.

Rows 13, 17 and 21 K15, *k2tog, yo twice, ssk, k16; rep from *, end last rep k15 (instead of 16).

Rows 15 and 19 K13, *[k2tog, yo twice, ssk] twice, k12; rep from * to last st, end k1.

Row 23 Knit.

Row 24 Purl.

Rep rows 1–24.

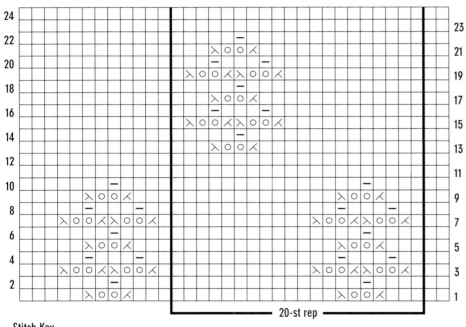

Stitch Key

- ☐ K on RS, p on WS
- ⊟ K on WS
- ⊙ Yo
- ╱ K2tog
- ╲ Ssk

allover

(multiple of 30 sts plus 19)

Row 1 (RS) K7, *k2tog, yo, k1, yo, k2tog, k25;
rep from *, end last rep k7 (instead of 25).

Row 2 P5, *k1, p2tog, yo, k3, yo, p2tog, k1,
p21; rep from *, end last rep p5 (instead of 21).

Row 3 Knit.

Row 4 P5, *k1, yo, p2tog, yo, p3tog, yo, p2tog,
yo, k1, p21; rep from *, end last rep p5 (instead of 21).

Row 5 K8, *p3, k27; rep from *, end last rep k8
(instead of 27).

Row 6 P6, *k2, yo, p3tog, yo, k2, p23; rep from *,
end last rep p6 (instead of 23).

Rows 7, 9 and 11 Knit.

Row 8 and all remaining WS rows Purl.

Row 13 K24, *yo, k2tog, k28; rep from *,
end last rep k23 (instead of 28).

Row 15 K22, *k2tog, yo, k1, yo, k2tog, k25;
rep from *, end last rep k22 (instead of 25).

Row 17 K21, *k2tog, yo, k3, yo, k2tog, k23;
rep from *, end last rep k21 (instead of 23).

Row 19 K21, *yo, k2tog, yo, k3tog, yo, k2tog,
yo, k23; rep from *, end last rep k21 (instead of 23).

Rows 21 and 23 Knit.

Row 24 Knit.

Rep rows 1–24.

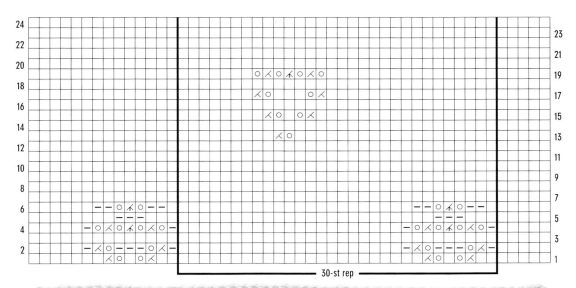

Stitch Key

□   K on RS, p on WS

─   P on RS, k on WS

○   Yo

╱   K2tog on RS, p2tog on WS

╱   K3tog on RS, p3tog on WS

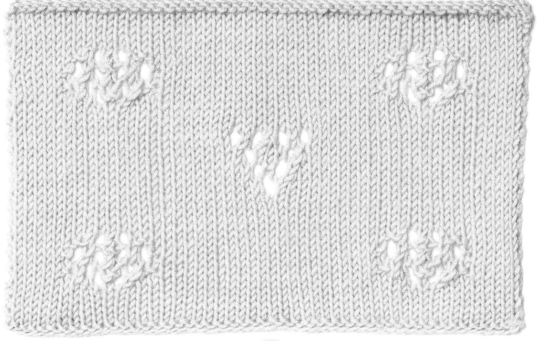

(multiple of 7 sts plus 2)
Rows 1, 3, 5, 7 and 9 (RS) *K2, yo, k1, yo, ssk, k2tog; rep from *, end k2.
Row 2 and all WS rows Purl.
Rows 11, 13, 15, 17 and 19 *K2, ssk, k2tog, yo, k1, yo; rep from *, end k2.
Row 20 Purl.
Rep rows 1–20.

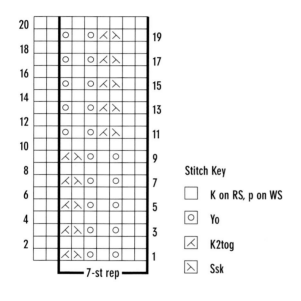

Stitch Key

☐	K on RS, p on WS
⊡	Yo
◸	K2tog
◹	Ssk

allover

(multiple of 10 sts plus 3)

Row 1 (RS) K1, p1, k1, *p5, k2tog, yo, k1, p1, k1; rep from * to end.
Row 2 and all WS rows K the knit sts and p the purl sts and yos.
Row 3 K1, p1, k1, *p4, k2tog, k1, yo, k1, p1, k1; rep from * to end.
Row 5 K1, p1, k1, *p3, k2tog, k2, yo, k1, p1, k1; rep from * to end.
Row 7 K1, p1, k1, *p2, k2tog, k3, yo, k1, p1, k1; rep from * to end.
Row 9 K1, p1, k1, *p1, k2tog, k4, yo, k1, p1, k1; rep from * to end.
Row 11 K1, p1, k1, *k2tog, k5, yo, k1, p1, k1; rep from * to end.

Row 13 K1, p1, k1, *yo, ssk, p5, k1, p1, k1; rep from * to end.
Row 15 K1, p1, k1, *yo, k1, ssk, p4, k1, p1, k1; rep from * to end.
Row 17 K1, p1, k1, *yo, k2, ssk, p3, k1, p1, k1; rep from * to end.
Row 19 K1, p1, k1, *yo, k3, ssk, p2, k1, p1, k1; rep from * to end.
Row 21 K1, p1, k1, *yo, k4, ssk, [p1, k1] twice; rep from * to end.
Row 23 K1, p1, k1, *yo, k5, ssk, k1, p1, k1; rep from * to end.
Row 24 Rep row 2.
Rep rows 1–24.

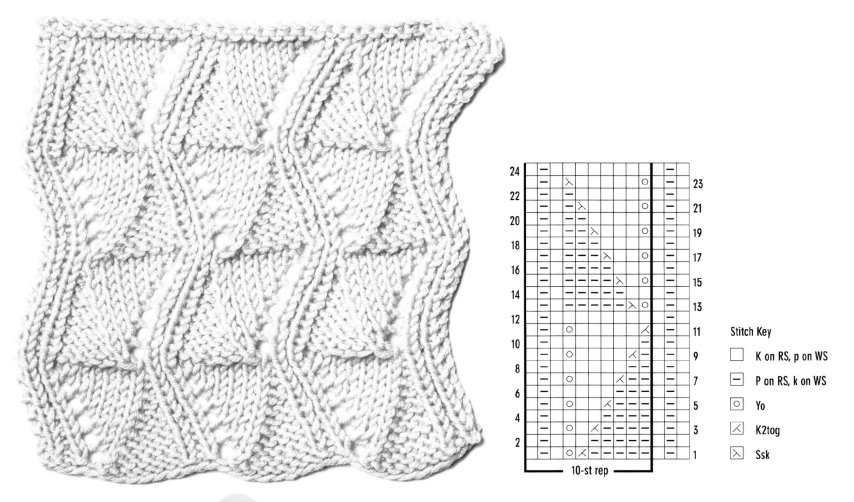

Stitch Key

☐ K on RS, p on WS

— P on RS, k on WS

⊡ Yo

◿ K2tog

◺ Ssk

(multiple of 10 sts plus 3)
Row 1 (RS) *Ssk, yo, k5, k2tog, yo, k1; rep from * to last 3 sts, end ssk, yo, k1.
Row 2 *P2tog, yo, p2, yo, p1, p2tog, p3; rep from * to last 3 sts, end p2tog, yo, p1.
Row 3 *Ssk, yo, k3, k2tog, k2, yo, k1; rep from * to last 3 sts, end ssk, yo, k1.
Row 4 *P2tog, yo, p2, yo, p3, p2tog, p1; rep from * to last 3 sts, end p2tog, yo, p1.
Row 5 *Ssk, yo, k2, ssk, k3, yo, k1; rep from * to last 3 sts, end ssk, yo, k1.
Row 6 *P2tog, yo, p2, yo, p3, ssp, p1; rep from * to last 3 sts, end p2tog, yo, p1.
Row 7 *Ssk, yo, k2, yo, ssk, k4; rep from * to last 3 sts, end ssk, yo, k1.
Row 8 *P2tog, yo, p4, ssp, p1, yo, p1; rep from * to last 3 sts, end p2tog, yo, p1.
Row 9 *Ssk, [yo, k2] twice, ssk, k2; rep from * to last 3 sts, end ssk, yo, k1.
Row 10 *P2tog, yo, p2, ssp, p3, yo, p1; rep from * to last 3 sts, end p2tog, yo, p1.
Row 11 *Ssk, yo, k2, yo, k3, k2tog, k1; rep from * to last 3 sts, end ssk, yo, k1.
Row 12 *P2tog, yo, p2, p2tog, p3, yo, p1; rep from * to last 3 sts, end p2tog, yo, p1.
Rep rows 1–12.

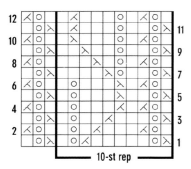

Stitch Key

☐ K on RS, p on WS

⊙ Yo

⊠ K2tog on RS, p2tog on WS

⊠ Ssk on RS, ssp on WS

82 vine and leaf

(multiple of 13 sts)
Row 1 (RS) *P1, k1, yo, k3, k2tog, k5, p1; rep from * to end.
Row 2 *K1, p5, p2tog, p2, yo, p2, k1; rep from * to end.
Row 3 *P1, k3, yo, k1, k2tog, k5, p1; rep from * to end.
Row 4 *K1, p5, p2tog, yo, p4, k1; rep from * to end.
Row 5 *P1, k5, ssk, k3, yo, k1, p1; rep from * to end.
Row 6 *K1, p2, yo, p2, ssp, p5, k1; rep from * to end.
Row 7 *P1, k5, ssk, k1, yo, k3, p1; rep from * to end.
Row 8 *K1, p4, yo, ssp, p5, k1; rep from * to end.
Rep rows 1–8.

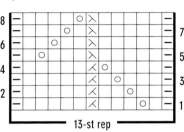

Stitch Key

- ☐ K on RS, p on WS
- ─ P on RS, k on WS
- ○ Yo
- ╱ K2tog on RS, p2tog on WS
- ╲ Ssk on RS, ssp on WS

13-st rep

83 crescent moons

(multiple of 14 sts plus 1)
Row 1 (RS) *K1, yo, k2tog, yo, k3, S2KP, k3, yo, ssk, yo; rep from *, end k1.
Row 2 and all WS rows Purl.
Row 3 *K1, yo, k2tog, k1, yo, k2, S2KP, k2, yo, k1, ssk, yo; rep from *, end k1.
Row 5 *K1, yo, k2tog, k2, yo, k1, S2KP, k1, yo, k2, ssk, yo; rep from *, end k1.
Row 7 *K1, yo, k2tog, k3, yo, S2KP, yo, k3, ssk, yo; rep from *, end k1.
Row 8 Purl.
Rep rows 1–8.

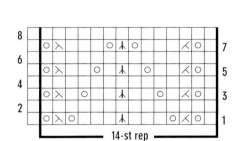

14-st rep

Stitch Key

- ☐ K on RS, p on WS
- ○ Yo
- ╱ K2tog
- ╲ Ssk
- ⅄ S2KP

allover

84 chinese fans

(multiple of 9 sts)
Row 1 (RS) Purl.
Row 2 Knit.
Row 3 *Ssk, yo, k1, yo, k4, k2tog; rep from * to end.
Rows 4, 6, 8 and 10 Purl.
Row 5 *Ssk, [k1, yo] twice, k3, k2tog; rep from * to end.

Row 7 *Ssk, k2, yo, k1, yo, k2, k2tog; rep from * to end.
Row 9 *Ssk, k3, [yo, k1] twice, k2tog; rep from * to end.
Row 11 *Ssk, k4, yo, k1, yo, k2tog; rep from * to end.
Row 12 Purl.
Rep rows 1–12.

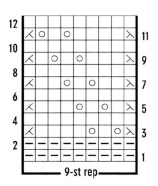

Stitch Key

☐	K on RS, p on WS
⊟	P on RS, k on WS
◌	Yo
◩	K2tog
◪	Ssk

85 footprints in the snow

(multiple of 10 sts plus 1)
Row 1 (RS) K2tog, *k3, yo, k1, yo, k3, SK2P; rep from *, end last rep k2tog (instead of SK2P).
Rows 2 and 4 Purl.
Row 3 K2tog, *k2, yo, k3, yo, k2, SK2P; rep from *, end last rep k2tog.

Row 5 K2tog, *[k1, yo] twice, SK2P, [yo, k1] twice, SK2P; rep from *, end last rep k2tog.
Row 6 Purl.
Rep rows 1–6.

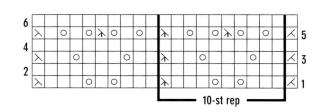

Stitch Key

☐	K on RS, p on WS
◌	Yo
◩	K2tog
◪	Ssk
⋏	SK2P

84

85

allover

(multiple of 16 sts plus 1)
Row 1 (RS) *K6, k2tog, yo, k1, yo, ssk, k5; rep from *, end k1.
Row 2 and all WS rows Purl.
Row 3 *K5, k2tog, yo, k3, yo, ssk, k4; rep from *, end k1.
Row 5 *K4, k2tog, yo, k5, yo ssk, k3; rep from *, end k1.
Row 7 *K3, k2tog, yo, k7, yo, ssk, k2; rep from *, end k1.
Row 9 *K2, k2tog, yo, k9, yo, ssk, k1; rep from *, end k1.
Row 11 *K1, k2tog, yo, k11, yo, ssk; rep from *, end k1.

Row 13 *K1, yo, ssk, k11, k2tog, yo; rep from *, end k1.
Row 15 *K2, yo, ssk, k9, k2tog, yo, k1; rep from *, end k1.
Row 17 *K3, yo, ssk, k7, k2tog, yo, k2; rep from *, end k1.
Row 19 *K4, yo, ssk, k5, k2tog, yo, k3; rep from *, end k1.
Row 21 *K5, yo, ssk, k3, k2tog, yo, k4; rep from *, end k1.
Row 23 *K6, yo, ssk, k1, k2tog, yo, k5; rep from *, end k1.
Row 24 Purl.
Rep rows 1–24.

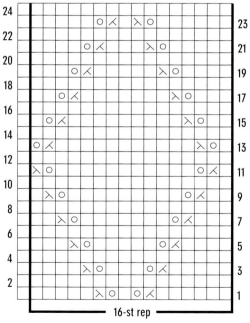

Stitch Key

	K on RS, p on WS
○	Yo
⋌	K2tog
⋋	Ssk

16-st rep

Ssk and pass Ssk, return resulting st to LH needle and pass 2nd st on LH needle over first st, then sl st back to RH needle.

(multiple of 22 sts plus 1)

Row 1 (RS) Ssk, yo, *k9, yo, ssk, k8, yo, SK2P, yo; rep from *, end last rep yo, k2tog (instead of yo, SK2P, yo).

Row 2 and all WS rows Purl.

Row 3 K1, *k1, yo, ssk, k5, k2tog, yo, k1, yo, ssk, k5, k2tog, yo, k2; rep from * to end.

Row 5 K1, *[yo, ssk] twice, k3, k2tog, yo, k3, yo, ssk, k3, [k2tog, yo] twice, k1; rep from * to end.

Row 7 K1, *k1, [yo, ssk] twice, k1, k2tog, yo, k5, yo, ssk, k1, [k2tog, yo] twice, k2; rep from * to end.

Row 9 K1, *[yo, ssk] twice, yo, SK2P, yo, k7, yo, SK2P, yo, [k2tog, yo] twice, k1; rep from * to end.

Row 11 K1, *k1, [yo, ssk] 3 times, k7, [k2tog, yo] 3 times, k2; rep from * to end.

Row 13 K1, *[yo, ssk] 4 times, k5, [k2tog, yo] 4 times, k1; rep from * to end.

Row 15 K1, *k1, [yo, ssk] 4 times, k3, [k2tog, yo] 4 times, k2; rep from * to end.

Row 17 K1, *[yo, ssk] 5 times, k1, [k2tog, yo] 5 times, k1; rep from * to end.

Row 19 K1, *k1, [yo, ssk] 3 times, yo, k2tog, yo, SK2P, yo, ssk, yo, [k2tog, yo] 3 times, k2; rep from * to end.

Row 21 K1, *[yo, ssk] 3 times, yo, ssk and pass, yo, k3, yo, SK2P, yo, [k2tog, yo] 3 times, k1; rep from * to end.

Row 23 K1, *k1, [yo, ssk] twice, yo, ssk and pass, yo, k5, yo, SK2P, yo, [k2tog, yo] twice, k2; rep from * to end.

Row 25 K1, *[yo, ssk] twice, yo, ssk and pass, yo, k7, yo, SK2P, yo, [k2tog, yo] twice, k1; rep from * to end.

Row 27 K1, *k1, yo, ssk, yo, ssk and pass, yo, k9, yo, SK2P, yo, k2tog, yo, k2; rep from * to end.

Row 29 K1, *yo, ssk, yo, ssk and pass, yo, k1, yo, ssk, k5, k2tog, yo, k1, yo, SK2P, yo, k2tog, yo, k1; rep from * to end.

Row 31 K1, *k1, yo, ssk and pass, yo, k3, yo, ssk, k3, k2tog, yo, k3, yo, SK2P, yo, k2; rep from * to end.

Row 33 K1, *yo, ssk and pass, yo, k5, yo, ssk, k1, k2tog, yo, k5, yo, SK2P, yo, k1; rep from * to end.

Row 35 K1, *k2tog, yo, k7, yo, SK2P, yo, k7, yo, ssk, k1; rep from * to end.

Row 36 Purl.

Rep rows 1–36.

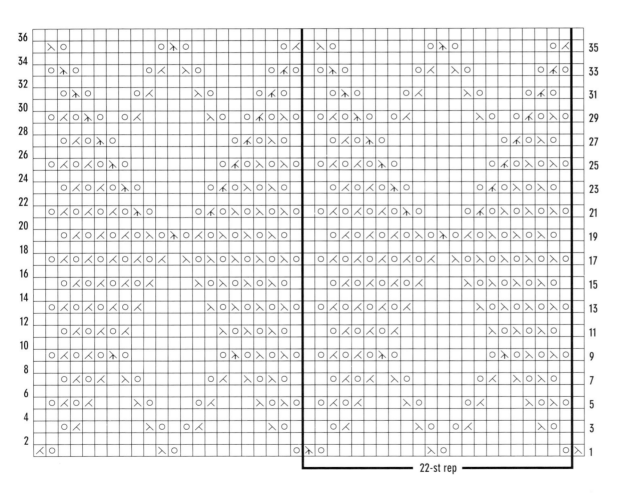

22-st rep

Stitch Key

- ☐ K on RS, p on WS
- ⊙ Yo
- ⟋ K2tog
- ⟍ Ssk
- ⼎ SK2P
- ⼎ Ssk and pass

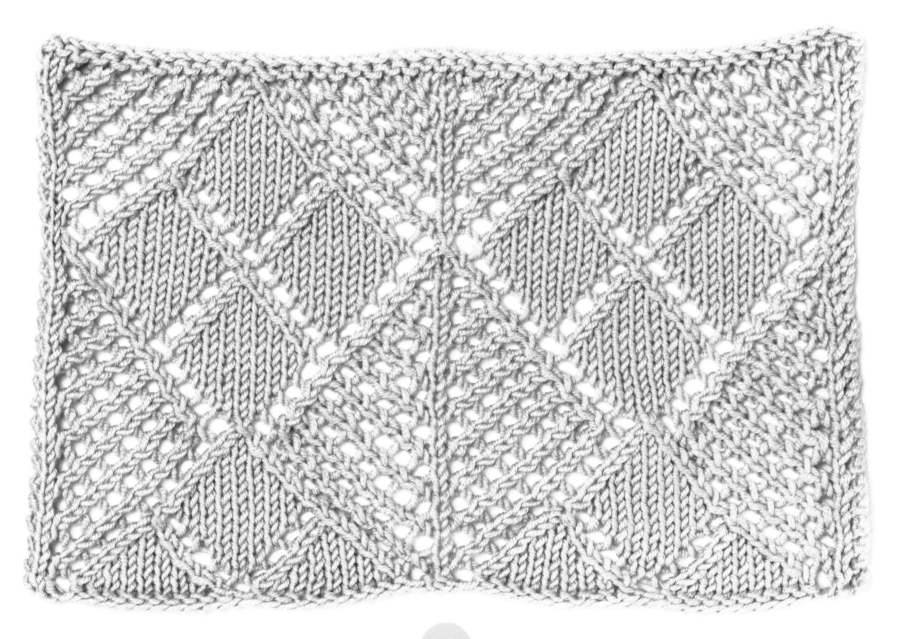

(multiple of 20 sts plus 3)

Row 1 (RS) K2, *[yo, ssk] 4 times, k3, [k2tog, yo] 4 times, k1; rep from *, end k1.

Row 2 and all WS rows Purl.

Row 3 K3, *[yo, ssk] 4 times, k1, [k2tog, yo] 4 times, k3; rep from * to end.

Row 5 K3, *k1, [yo, ssk] 3 times, yo, SK2P, yo, [k2tog, yo] 3 times, k4; rep from * to end.

Row 7 K3, *k2, [yo, ssk] 3 times, k1, [k2tog, yo] 3 times, k5; rep from * to end.

Row 9 K3, *k3, [yo, ssk] twice, yo, SK2P, yo, [k2tog, yo] twice, k6; rep from * to end.

Row 11 K2, *yo, ssk, k3, [yo, ssk] twice, k1, [k2tog, yo] twice, k3, k2tog, yo, k1; rep from *, end k1.

Row 13 K3, *yo, ssk, k3, yo, ssk, yo, SK2P, yo, k2tog, yo, k3, k2tog, yo, k3; rep from * to end.

Row 15 K2, k2tog, yo, k1, yo, ssk, k2, yo, ssk, *k1, k2tog, yo, k2, k2tog, yo, k1, yo, ssk, yo, k3tog, yo, k1, yo, ssk, k2, yo, ssk; rep from * to last 12 sts, end k1, k2tog, yo, k2, k2tog, yo, k1, yo, ssk, k2.

Row 17 K1, k2tog, yo, k3, yo, ssk, k2, *yo, SK2P, yo, k2, k2tog, yo, k3, yo, SK2P, yo, k3, yo, ssk, k2; rep from * to last 13 sts, end yo, SK2P, yo, k2, k2tog, yo, k3, yo, ssk, k1.

Row 19 K4, yo, k3tog, yo, k2, k2tog, yo, *k1, yo, ssk, k2, yo, SK2P, yo, k2, yo, ssk, k1, yo, k3tog, yo, k2, k2tog, yo; rep from * to last 12 sts, end k1, yo, ssk, k2, yo, SK2P, yo, k4.

Row 21 K3, yo, k3tog, yo, k2, k2tog, yo, k1, *k2, yo, ssk, k2, yo, SK2P, yo, k3, yo, k3tog, yo, k2, k2tog, yo, k1; rep from * to last 12 sts, end k2, yo, ssk, k2, yo, SK2P, yo, k3.

Row 23 K1, yo, k3tog, yo, k3, [k2tog, yo] twice, *k1, [yo, ssk] twice, k3, yo, ssk, yo, k3tog, yo, k3, [k2tog, yo] twice; rep from * to last 12 sts, end k1, [yo, ssk] twice, k3, yo, SK2P, yo, k1.

Row 25 K1, k2tog, yo, k3, [k2tog, yo] twice, k1, *k2, [yo, ssk] twice, k3, yo, SK2P, yo, k3, [k2tog, yo] twice, k1; rep from * to last 12 sts, end k2, [yo, ssk] twice, k3, yo, ssk, k1.

Row 27 *K5, [k2tog, yo] 3 times, k1, [yo, ssk] 3 times, k2; rep from *, end k3.

Row 29 *K4, [k2tog, yo] 3 times, k3, [yo, ssk] 3 times, k1; rep from *, end k3.

Row 31 K3, *[k2tog, yo] 4 times, k1, [yo, ssk] 4 times, k3; rep from * to end.

Row 33 K1, *k1, [k2tog, yo] 4 times, k3, [yo, ssk] 4 times; rep from *, end k2.

Row 35 K1, [k2tog, yo] 4 times, k2, *k3, [yo, ssk] 3 times, yo, SK2P, yo, [k2tog, yo] 3 times, k2; rep from * to last 12 sts, end k3, [yo, ssk] 4 times, k1.

Row 36 Purl.

Rep rows 1–36.

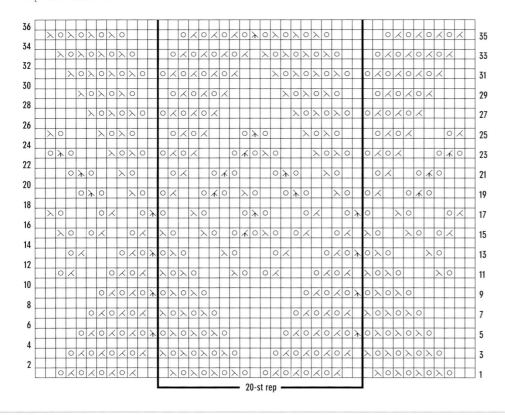

Stitch Key

☐ K on RS, p on WS

○ Yo

╱ K2tog

╲ Ssk

⋌ K3tog

⋏ SK2P

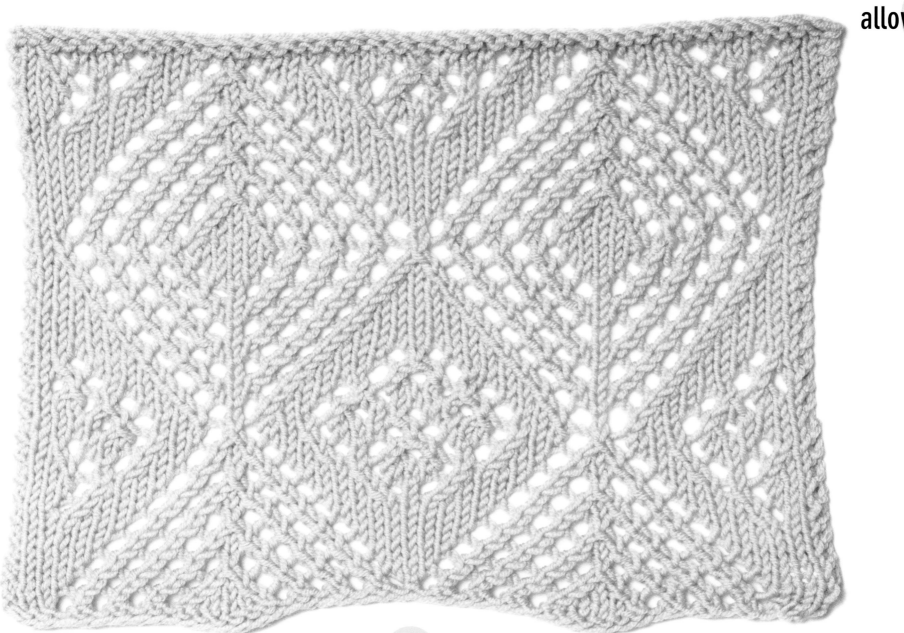

88

(multiple of 22 sts plus 1)

Row 1 (RS) K1, *yo, ssk, [p2, k1 tbl] 5 times, p2, k2tog, yo, k1; rep from * to end.

Row 2 *P2, yo, p2tog, k1, [p1 tbl, k2] 4 times, p1 tbl, k1, ssp, yo, p1; rep from *, end p1.

Row 3 K1, *k2, yo, ssk, k1 tbl, [p2, k1 tbl] 4 times, k2tog, yo, k3; rep from * to end.

Row 4 *[P1, yo, p2tog] twice, k2, [p1 tbl, k2] 3 times, ssp, yo, p1, ssp, yo; rep from *, end p1.

Row 5 K1, *[k1, yo, ssk] twice, p1, [k1 tbl, p2] twice, k1 tbl, p1, [k2tog, yo, k1] twice, k1; rep from * to end.

Row 6 *P2, [p1, yo, p2tog] twice, [p1 tbl, k2] twice, p1 tbl, [ssp, yo, p1] twice, p1; rep from *, end p1.

Row 7 K1, *[yo, ssk, k1] twice, yo, ssk, p2, k1 tbl, p2, [k2tog, yo, k1] 3 times; rep from * to end.

Row 8 *P1, [p1, yo, p2tog] 3 times, k1, p1 tbl, k1, [ssp, yo, p1] 3 times; rep from *, end p1.

Row 9 K1, *k2, [yo, ssk, k1] twice, yo, ssk, k1 tbl, [k2tog, yo, k1] 3 times, k2; rep from * to end.

Row 10 *P4, [yo, p2tog, p1] twice, yo, sssp, yo, [p1, ssp, yo] twice, p3; rep from *, end p1.

Row 11 K1 tbl, *[p2, k1 tbl] twice, p2, k2tog, yo, k1, yo, ssk, [p2, k1 tbl] 3 times; rep from * to end.

Row 12 *[P1 tbl, k2] twice, p1 tbl, k1, ssp, yo, p3, yo, p2tog, k1, [p1 tbl, k2] twice; rep from *, end p1 tbl.

Row 13 K1 tbl, *[p2, k1 tbl] twice, k2tog, yo, k5, yo, ssk, [k1 tbl, p2] twice, k1 tbl; rep from * to end.

Row 14 *[P1 tbl, k2] twice, [ssp, yo, p1] twice, yo, p2tog, p1, yo, p2tog, k2, p1 tbl, k2; rep from *, end p1 tbl.

Row 15 K1 tbl, *p2, k1 tbl, p1, [k2tog, yo, k1] twice, k2, yo, ssk, k1, yo, ssk, p1, k1 tbl, p2, k1 tbl; rep from * to end.

Row 16 *P1 tbl, k2, p1 tbl, [ssp, yo, p1] twice, p4, yo, p2tog, p1, yo, p2tog, p1 tbl, k2; rep from *, end p1 tbl.

Row 17 K1 tbl, *p2, [k2tog, yo, k1] 3 times, [yo, ssk, k1] twice, yo, ssk, p2, k1 tbl; rep from * to end.

Row 18 *P1 tbl, k1, [ssp, yo, p1] 3 times, p2, [yo, p2tog, p1] twice, yo, p2tog, k1; rep from *, end p1 tbl.

Row 19 K1 tbl, *[k2tog, yo, k1] 3 times, k4, [yo, ssk, k1] twice, yo, ssk, k1 tbl; rep from * to end.

Row 20 [Ssp, yo, p1] 3 times, p6, [yo, p2tog, p1] twice, yo, *sssp, yo, [p1, ssp, yo] twice, p7, [yo, p2tog, p1] twice, yo; rep from *, end p2tog.

Rep rows 1–20.

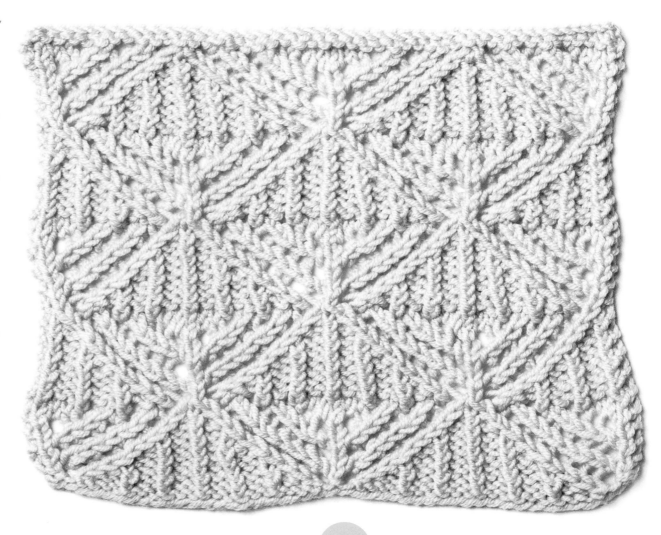

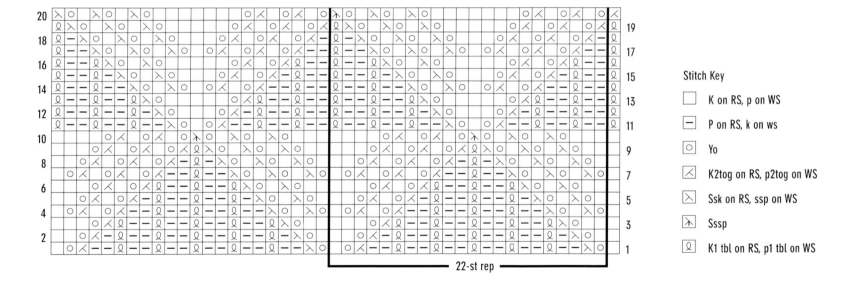

22-st rep

Stitch Key

☐ K on RS, p on WS

─ P on RS, k on ws

○ Yo

╱ K2tog on RS, p2tog on WS

╲ Ssk on RS, ssp on WS

⅄ Sssp

Ω K1 tbl on RS, p1 tbl on WS

90 color stripes

(worked over an odd number of sts)
Row 1 (RS) With CC, *p1, k1; rep from *, end p1.
Row 2 Rep row 1.
Rows 3, 5, 6 and 7 With MC, rep row 1.
Rows 4 and 8 With MC, p1, *yo, p2tog; rep from * to end.
Rows 9 and 10 With CC, rep row 1.
Rows 11 and 12 With MC, rep row 1.
Rep rows 1–12.

Color Key

☐ MC

▨ CC

Stitch Key

☐ K on RS, p on WS

⊟ P on RS, k on WS

⊙ Yo

◿ P2tog

91 tiny daisies

Daisy St P3tog, but do not remove sts from LH needle, yo, p3tog again and drop sts from needle.
(multiple of 4 sts plus 1)
Rows 1 and 3 (RS) Knit.
Row 2 K1, *Daisy St, k1; rep from * to end.
Row 4 K1, p1, *k1, Daisy St; rep from *, end k1, p1, k1.
Rep rows 1–4.

Stitch Key

☐ K on RS, p on WS

⊟ K on WS

▨ Daisy Stitch

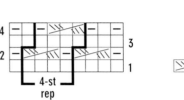

92 perforated diamonds

(multiple of 6 sts plus 1)
Row 1 (RS) K1, *yo, ssk, k1, k2tog, yo, k1; rep from * to end.
Rows 2, 4 and 6 Purl.
Row 3 K1, *k1, yo, S2KP, yo, k2; rep from * to end.
Row 5 K1, *k2tog, yo, k1, yo, ssk, k1; rep from * to end.
Row 7 K2tog, *yo, k3, yo, S2KP; rep from *, end last rep ssk (instead of S2KP).
Row 8 Purl.
Rep rows 1–8.

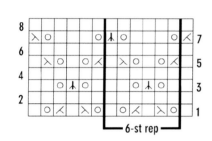

Stitch Key

☐ K on RS, p on WS

◯ Yo

╱ K2tog

╲ Ssk

⅄ S2KP

93 snow flurry

(multiple of 8 sts plus 1)
Row 1 (RS) K1, *ssk, [k1, yo] twice, k1, k2tog, k1; rep from * to end.
Rows 2, 4 and 6 Purl.
Row 3 K1, *ssk, yo, k3, yo, k2tog, k1; rep from * to end.
Row 5 K1, *yo, k1, k2tog, k1, ssk, k1, yo, k1; rep from * to end.
Row 7 K1, *k1, yo, k2tog, k1, ssk, yo, k2; rep from * to end.
Row 8 Purl.
Rep rows 1–8.

allover

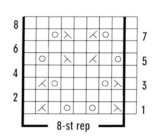

Stitch Key

☐ K on RS, p on WS

◯ Yo

╱ K2tog

╲ Ssk

(multiple of 10 sts plus 5)
Note Sl sts purlwise wyif.
Rows 1 and 3 (RS) *K2tog, yo, k1, yo, ssk, k5;
rep from * to last 5 sts,
end k2tog, yo, k1, yo, ssk.
Rows 2 and 4 P2, *sl 1, p9; rep from *, end sl 1, p2.
Row 5 Knit.

Row 6 Purl.
Rows 7 and 9 *K5, k2tog, yo, k1, yo, ssk; rep from
*, end k5.
Rows 8 and 10 P5, *p2, sl 1, p7; rep from * to end.
Row 11 Knit.
Row 12 Purl.
Rep rows 1–12.

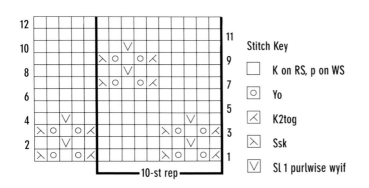

Stitch Key

	K on RS, p on WS
	Yo
	K2tog
	Ssk
	Sl 1 purlwise wyif

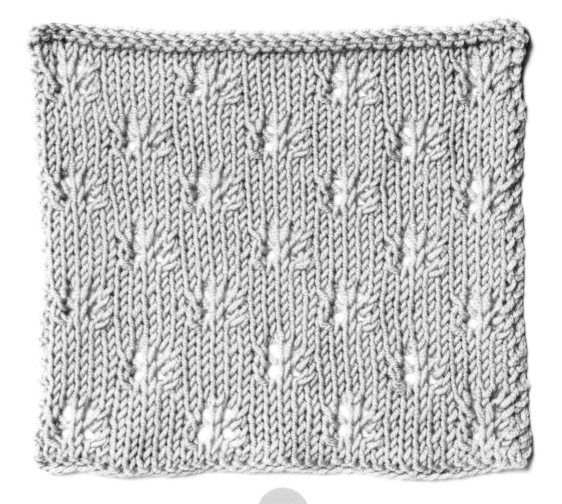

94

allover

95

(multiple of 6 sts plus 3)

Row 1 (RS) P3, *k3, yo, p3; rep from * to end.

Row 2 K3, *p4, k3; rep from * to end.

Row 3 P3, *k1, k2tog, yo, k1, p3; rep from * to end.

Row 4 K3, *p2, p2tog, k3; rep from * to end.

Row 5 P3, *k1, yo, k2tog, p3; rep from * to end.

Row 6 K3, *p3, k3; rep from * to end.

Rep rows 1–6.

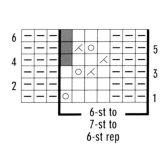

Stitch Key

☐ K on RS, p on WS

☐ P on RS, k on WS

☐ Yo

☑ K2tog on RS, p2tog on WS

▨ No stitch

96

(multiple of 11 sts)

Row 1 (RS) *K3, k2tog, yo, k1, yo, ssk, k3; rep from * to end.

Rows 2, 4 and 6 Purl.

Row 3 *K2, k2tog, yo, k3, yo, ssk, k2; rep from * to end.

Row 5 *K1, [k2tog, yo] twice, k1, [yo, ssk] twice, k1; rep from * to end.

Row 7 *[K2tog, yo] twice, k3, [yo, ssk] twice; rep from * to end.

Row 8 Purl.

Rep rows 1–8.

Stitch Key

☐ K on RS, p on WS

☐ Yo

☑ K2tog

☒ Ssk

(multiple of 10 sts plus 3)

Row 1 (RS) K1, *yo, ssk, k8; rep from *, end yo, ssk.

Row 2 and all WS rows Purl.

Row 3 K1, *k1, yo, ssk, k5, k2tog, yo; rep from *, end k2.

Row 5 K1, *k2, yo, ssk, k3, k2tog,
yo, k1; rep from *, end k2.

Row 7 Rep row 3.

Row 9 K1, *k5, yo, ssk, k3; rep from *, end k2.

Row 11 K1, *k3, k2tog, yo, k1, yo, ssk, k2; rep from *, end k2.

Row 13 K1, *k2, k2tog, yo, k3, yo, ssk, k1; rep from *, end k2.

Row 15 Rep row 11.

Row 16 Purl.

Rep rows 1–16.

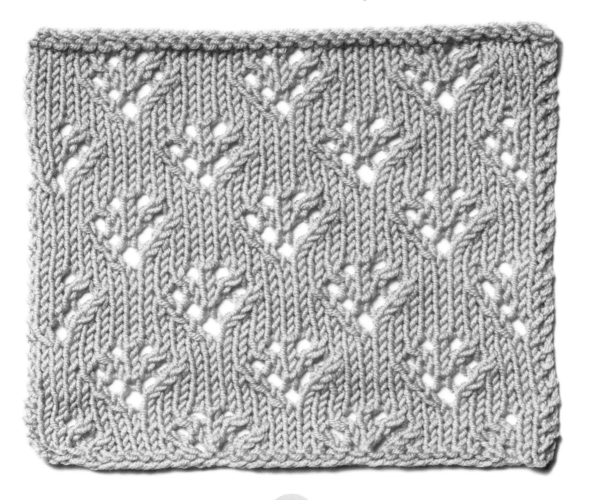

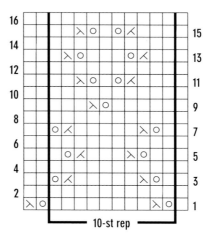

Stitch Key

☐ K on RS, p on WS

◯ Yo

K2tog

Ssk

10-st rep

allover

(multiple of 10 sts plus 3)
Row 1 (RS) Knit.
Row 2 Purl.
Row 3 K1, *p1, k3, yo, SK2P, yo, k3; rep from *, end p1, k1.
Row 4 P2, *k1, p7, k1, p1; rep from *, end p1.

Row 5 K1, *k2, p1, k2, yo, k2tog, k1, p1, k1; rep from *, end k2.
Row 6 P2, *p2, k1, p3, k1, p3; rep from *, end p1.
Row 7 K1, *yo, ssk, k2, p1, k1, p1, k3; rep from *, end yo, ssk.
Row 8 P2, *p4, k1, p5; rep from *, end p1.
Rep rows 1–8.

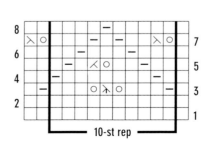

Stitch Key

☐ K on RS, p on WS

⊟ P on RS, k on WS

◯ Yo

╱ K2tog

╲ Ssk

⋀ SK2P

Cockleshell Stitch [Sl 1 purlwise, drop double yo from LH needle without working it] 14 times, sl 1 purlwise (15 long loops on RH needle); sl loops back to LH needle and purl all 15 loops tog.
(begin on a multiple of 19 sts plus 4)
Row 1 (RS) Knit.
Row 2 K3, *yo twice, k2tog, k13, k2tog, yo twice, k2; rep from *, end k1.

Row 3 K3, *[k1, p1] into double yo, k15, [k1, p1] into double yo, k2; rep from *, end k1.
Rows 4 and 5 Knit.
Row 6 K3, *[yo twice, k2tog] twice, k11, [k2tog, yo twice] twice, k2; rep from *, end k1.
Row 7 K3, *[(k1, p1) into double yo, k1] twice, k12, [(k1, p1) into double yo, k1] twice, k1; rep from *, end k1.
Row 8 Knit.

Row 9 K8, *[yo twice, k1] 14 times, k11; rep from *, end last rep k7 (instead of 11).
Row 10 K3, *[yo twice, k2tog] twice, yo twice, work Cockleshell St, [yo twice, k2tog] twice, yo twice, k2; rep from *, end k1.
Row 11 K3, *[(k1, p1) into double yo, k1] 5 times, [k1 p1] into double yo, k2; rep from *, end k1.
Row 12 Knit.
Rep rows 1–12.

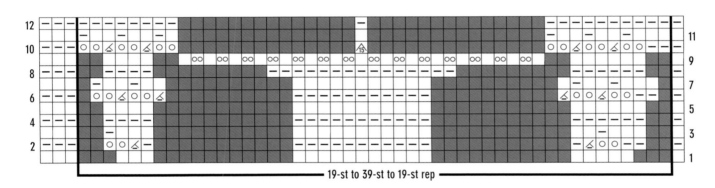

■■■ 19-st to 39-st to 19-st rep ■■■

Stitch Key

⬜ K on RS

⊟ P on RS, k on WS

◿ K2tog on WS

|o|o| Yo twice on WS (on RS row above double yo, work k1, p1 into double yo)

|oo| Yo twice on RS (on WS row above double yo, work Cockleshell Stitch as directed)

◸15 Cockleshell Stitch

■ No stitch

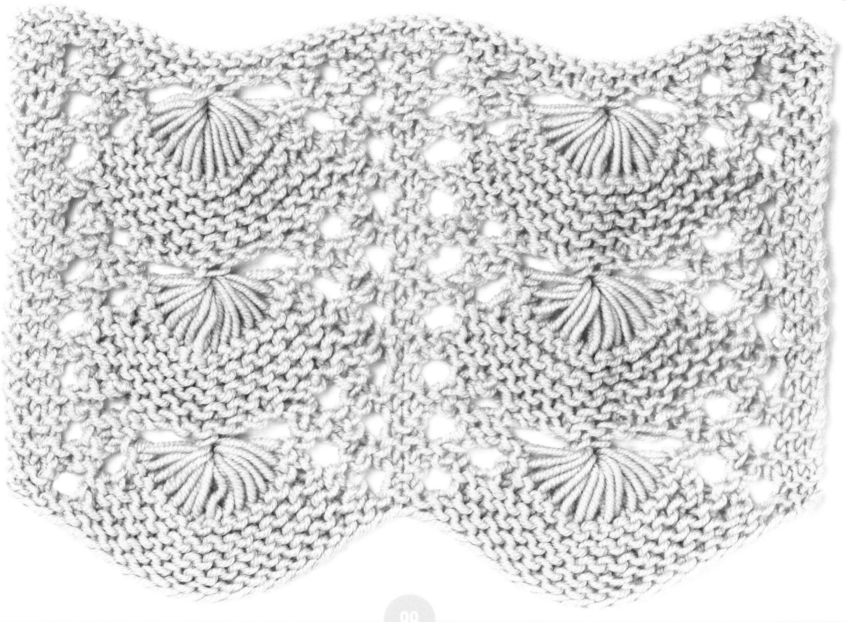

(multiple of 8 sts plus 1)

Rows 1, 3, 5 and 7 (RS) P1, *[k1, p2] twice, k1, p1; rep from * to end.

Rows 2, 4, 6 and 8 *K1, [p1, k2] twice, p1; rep from *, end k1.

Row 9 P1, *M1 purl, ssk, p1, k1, p1, k2tog, M1 purl, p1; rep from * to end.

Row 10 *K2, [p1, k1] 3 times; rep from *, end k1.

Row 11 P1, *p1, M1 purl, ssk, k1, k2tog, M1 purl, p2; rep from * to end.

Row 12 *K3, p3, k2; rep from *, end k1.

Row 13 P1, *p2, M1 purl, S2KP, M1 purl, p3; rep from * to end.

Rows 14, 16, 18 and 20 *P2, [k1, p1] 3 times; rep from *, end p1.

Rows 15, 17 and 19 K2tog, *yo, [p1, k1] twice, p1, yo, S2KP; rep from *, end last rep ssk (instead of S2KP).

Row 21 K1, *p1, k2tog, M1 purl, p1, M1 purl, ssk, p1, k1; rep from * to end.

Row 22 *P1, k1, p1, k3, p1, k1; rep from *, end p1.

Row 23 K1, *k2tog, M1 purl, p3, M1 purl, ssk, k1; rep from * to end.

Row 24 *P2, k5, p1; rep from *, end p1.

Row 25 K2tog, *M1 purl, p5, M1 purl, S2KP; rep from *, end last rep ssk.

Row 26 Rep row 2.

Rep rows 1–26.

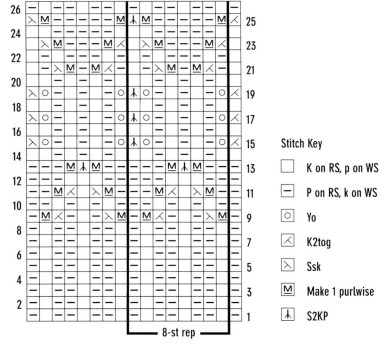

Stitch Key

☐	K on RS, p on WS
−	P on RS, k on WS
○	Yo
╱	K2tog
╲	Ssk
M	Make 1 purlwise
⋏	S2KP

8-st rep

allover

(multiple of 10 sts plus 1)

Row 1 (RS) Ssk, *k3, yo, k1, yo, k3, S2KP; rep from *, end last rep k2tog (instead of S2KP).

Row 2 and all WS rows Purl.

Row 3 Ssk, *k2, yo, k3, yo, k2, S2KP; rep from *, end last rep k2tog.

Row 5 Ssk, *k1, yo, k5, yo, k1, S2KP; rep from *, end last rep k2tog.

Row 7 Ssk, *yo, k7, yo, S2KP; rep from *, end last rep k2tog.

Row 9 K1, *yo, k3, S2KP, k3, yo, k1; rep from * to end.

Row 11 K1, *k1, yo, k2, S2KP, k2, yo, k2; rep from * to end.

Row 13 K1, *k2, yo, k1, S2KP, k1, yo, k3; rep from * to end.

Row 15 K1, *k3, yo, S2KP, yo, k4;

rep from * to end.

Row 16 Purl.

Rep rows 1–16.

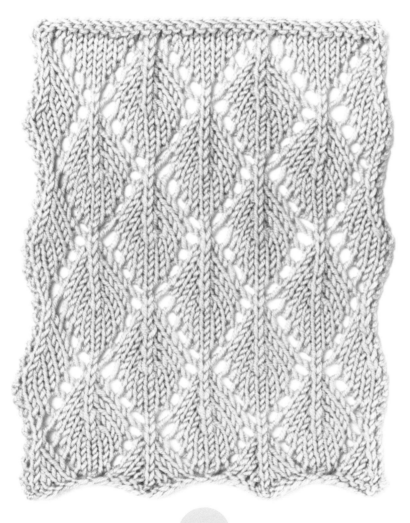

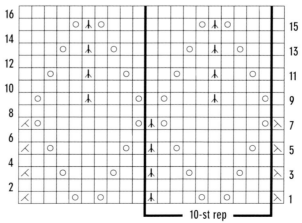

Stitch Key

☐	K on RS, p on WS
⊙	Yo
╱	K2tog
╲	Ssk
⅄	S2KP

10-st rep

(multiple of 14 sts plus 1)
Row 1 (RS) K1, *yo, k2, p3, p3tog, p3, k2, yo, k1; rep from * to end.
Row 2 P1, *p3, k7, p4; rep from * to end.
Row 3 K1, *k1, yo, k2, p2, p3tog, p2, k2, yo, k2; rep from * to end.
Row 4 P1, *p4, k5, p5; rep from * to end.
Row 5 K1, *k2, yo, k2, p1, p3tog, p1, k2, yo, k3; rep from * to end.
Row 6 P1, *p5, k3, p6; rep from * to end.

Row 7 K1, *k3, yo, k2, p3tog, k2, yo, k4; rep from * to end.
Row 8 P1, *p6, k1, p7; rep from * to end.
Row 9 P2tog, *p3, k2, yo, k1, yo, k2, p3, p3tog; rep from *, end last rep p2tog (instead of p3tog).
Row 10 K1, *k3, p7, k4; rep from * to end.
Row 11 P2tog, *p2, k2, yo, k3, yo, k2, p2, p3tog; rep from *, end last rep p2tog.

Row 12 K1, *k2, p9, k3; rep from * to end.
Row 13 P2tog, *p1, k2, yo, k5, yo, k2, p1, p3tog; rep from *, end last rep p2tog.
Row 14 K1, *k1, p11, k2; rep from * to end.
Row 15 P2tog, *k2, yo, k7, yo, k2, p3tog; rep from *, end last rep p2tog.
Row 16 K1, *p13, k1; rep from * to end.
Rep rows 1–16.

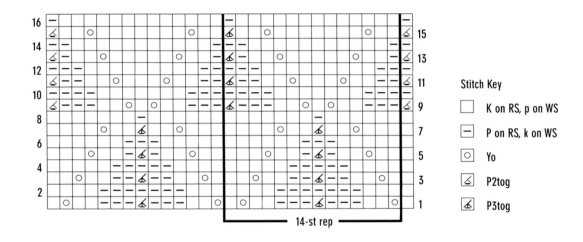

14-st rep

Stitch Key

☐	K on RS, p on WS
⊟	P on RS, k on WS
⊙	Yo
◿	P2tog
◢	P3tog

(multiple of 8 sts plus 3)

Rows 1, 3, 5 and 7 (RS) K1, k2tog, k2, yo, k1, yo, *k2, k3tog, k2, yo, k1, yo; rep from * to last 5 sts, end k2, ssk, k1.

Row 2 and all WS rows Purl.

Rows 9, 11, 13 and 15 K1, yo, k1, *k2, k3tog, k2, yo, k1, yo; rep from * to last 9 sts, end k2, k3tog, k3, yo, k1.

Row 16 Purl.

Rep rows 1–16.

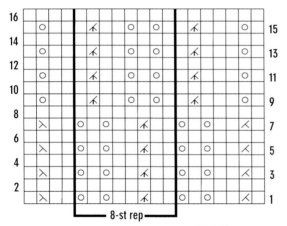

8-st rep

Stitch Key

☐	K on RS, p on WS
⊙	Yo
╱	K2tog
╲	Ssk
⅄	K3tog

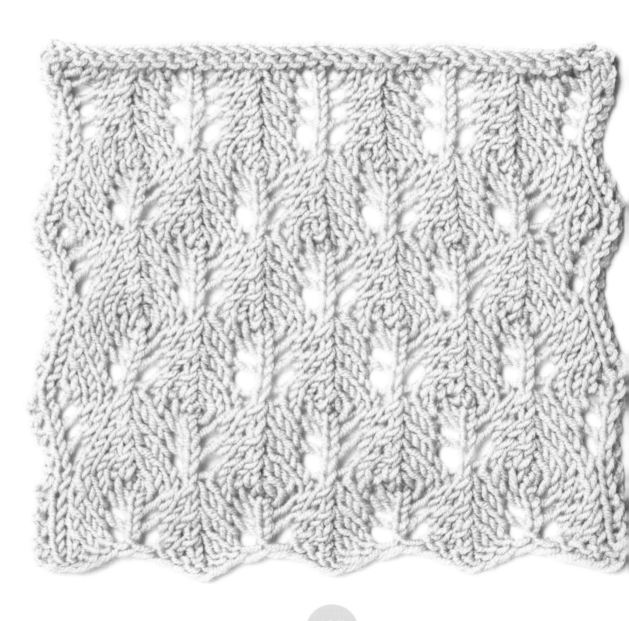

allover

(multiple of 10 sts plus 1)

Row 1 (RS) K1, *k1, k2tog, [k1, yo] twice, k1, ssk, k2; rep from * to end.
Row 2 and all WS rows Purl.
Row 3 K1, *k2tog, k1, yo, k3, yo, k1, ssk, k1; rep from * to end.
Row 5 K2tog, *k1, yo, k5, yo, k1, SK2P; rep from *, end last rep ssk (instead of SK2P).
Row 7 K1, *k1, yo, k1, ssk, k1, k2tog, k1, yo, k2; rep from * to end.
Row 9 K1, *k1, yo, k2, SK2P, k2, yo, k2; rep from * to end.
Row 11 K1, *yo, k1, ssk, k3, k2tog, k1, yo, k1; rep from * to end.
Row 13 K1, *k1, yo, k1, ssk, k1, k2tog, k1, yo, k2; rep from * to end.
Row 15 K1, *k2, yo, k1, SK2P, k1, yo, k3; rep from * to end.
Row 17 K1, *k2tog, k1, yo, k3, yo, k1, ssk, k1; rep from * to end.
Row 19 K2tog, *k2, yo, k3, yo, k2, SK2P; rep from *, end last rep ssk.
Row 20 Purl.
Rep rows 1–20.

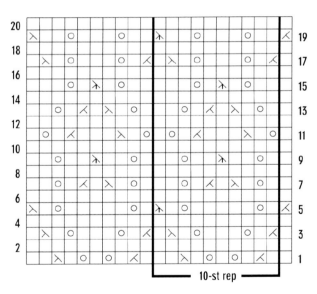

10-st rep

Stitch Key

☐ K on RS, p on WS

◉ Yo

╱ K2tog

╲ Ssk

⅄ SK2P

(multiple of 18 sts plus 3)

Row 1 (RS) P1, k1 tbl, *yo, p2, [k1 tbl] twice, p3, p3tog, p3, [k1 tbl] twice, p2, yo, k1 tbl; rep from *, end p1.

Row 2 K1, *p1 tbl, p1, k2, [p1 tbl] twice, k7, [p1 tbl] twice, k2, p1; rep from *, end p1 tbl, k1.

Row 3 P1, k1 tbl, *yo, k1 tbl, p2, [k1 tbl] twice, p2, p3tog, p2, [k1 tbl] twice, p2, k1 tbl, yo, k1 tbl; rep from *, end p1.

Row 4 K1, *p1 tbl, p1, p1 tbl, k2, [p1 tbl] twice, k5, [p1 tbl] twice, k2, p1 tbl, p1; rep from *, end p1 tbl, k1.

Row 5 P1, k1 tbl, *yo, [k1 tbl] twice, p2, [k1 tbl] twice, p1, p3tog, p1, [k1 tbl] twice, p2, [k1 tbl] twice, yo, k1 tbl; rep from *, end p1.

Row 6 K1, *p1 tbl, p1, [p1 tbl] twice, k2, [p1 tbl] twice, k3, [p1 tbl] twice, k2, [p1 tbl] twice, p1; rep from *, end p1 tbl, k1.

Row 7 P1, k1 tbl, *yo, p1, [k1 tbl] twice, p2, [k1 tbl] twice, p3tog, [k1 tbl] twice, p2, [k1 tbl] twice, p1, yo, k1 tbl; rep from *, end p1.

Row 8 K1, *p1 tbl, p1, k1, [(p1 tbl) twice, k2, (p1 tbl) twice, k1] twice, p1; rep from *, end p1 tbl, k1.

Row 9 P1, k1 tbl, *yo, p2, [k1 tbl] twice, p2, k1 tbl, k3tog tbl, k1 tbl, p2, [k1 tbl] twice, p2, yo, k1 tbl; rep from *, end p1.

Row 10 K1, *p1 tbl, p1, k2, [p1 tbl] twice, k2, [p1 tbl] 3 times, k2, [p1 tbl] twice, k2, p1; rep from *, end p1 tbl, k1.

Row 11 P1, k1 tbl, *yo, p3, [k1 tbl] twice, p2, k3tog tbl, p2, [k1 tbl] twice, p3, yo, k1 tbl; rep from *, end p1.

Row 12 K1, *p1 tbl, p1, k3, [p1 tbl] twice, k2, p1 tbl, k2, [p1 tbl] twice, k3, p1; rep from *, end p1 tbl, k1.

Row 13 P1, p2tog, *p3, [k1 tbl] twice, p2, yo, k1 tbl, yo, p2, [k1 tbl] twice, p3, p3tog; rep from *, end last rep p2tog, p1 (instead of p3tog).

Row 14 K1, *k4, [p1 tbl] twice, k2, p1, p1 tbl, p1, k2, [p1 tbl] twice, k3; rep from *, end k2.

Row 15 P1, p2tog, *p2, [k1 tbl] twice, p2, [k1 tbl, yo] twice, k1 tbl, p2, [k1 tbl] twice, p2, p3tog; rep from *, end last rep p2tog, p1 (instead of p3tog).

Row 16 K1, *k3, [p1 tbl] twice, k2, [p1 tbl, p1] twice, p1 tbl, k2, [p1 tbl] twice, k2; rep from *, end k2.

Row 17 P1, p2tog, *p1, [k1 tbl] twice, p2, [k1 tbl] twice, [yo, k1 tbl] twice, k1 tbl, p2, [k1 tbl] twice, p1, p3tog; rep from *, end last rep p2tog, p1 (instead of p3tog).

Row 18 K1, *[k2, (p1 tbl) twice] twice, [p1, p1 tbl] twice, p1 tbl, k2, [p1 tbl] twice, k1; rep from *, end k2.

Row 19 P1, p2tog, *[k1 tbl] twice, p2, [k1 tbl] twice, p1, yo, k1 tbl, yo, p1, [k1 tbl] twice, p2, [k1 tbl] twice, p3tog; rep from *, end last rep p2tog, p1 (instead of p3tog).

Row 20 K1, *k1, [p1 tbl] twice, k2, [p1 tbl] twice, k1, p1, p1 tbl, p1, k1, [p1 tbl] twice, k2, [p1 tbl] twice; rep from *, end k2.

Row 21 P1, k2tog tbl, *k1 tbl, p2, [k1 tbl] twice, p2, yo, k1 tbl, yo, p2, [k1 tbl] twice, p2, k1 tbl, k3tog tbl; rep from *, end last rep k2tog tbl, p1 (instead of k3tog tbl).

Row 22 K1, *[(p1 tbl) twice, k2] twice, p1, p1 tbl, p1, k2, [p1 tbl] twice, k2, p1 tbl; rep from *, end p1 tbl, k1.

Row 23 P1, k2tog tbl, *p2, [k1 tbl] twice, p3, yo, k1 tbl, yo, p3, [k1 tbl] twice, p2, k3tog tbl; rep from *, end last rep k2tog tbl, p1 (instead of k3tog tbl).

Row 24 K1, *p1 tbl, k2, [p1 tbl] twice, k3, p1, p1 tbl, p1, k3, [p1 tbl] twice, k2; rep from *, end p1 tbl, k1.

Rep rows 1–24.

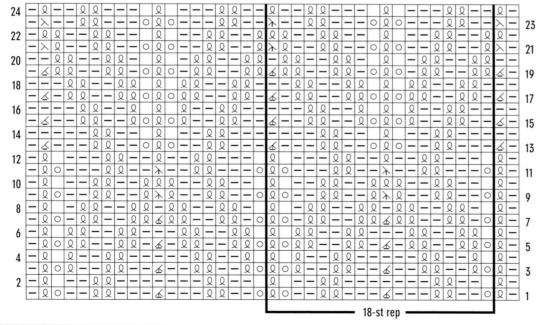

Stitch Key

☐ K on RS, p on WS

— P on RS, k on WS

⊡ Yo

⧄ K2tog tbl

⧅ P2tog

⋏ K3tog tbl

⧄ P3tog

 Q K1 tbl on RS, p1 tbl on WS

18-st rep

(multiple of 16 sts)
Row 1 (WS) *P7 tbl, p1, p2 tbl, k1, p2 tbl, p1, p2 tbl; rep from * to end.
Row 2 *K2 tbl, k2tog, p1, k1, p1, ssk, k4 tbl, yo, k1 tbl, yo, k2 tbl; rep from * to end.
Row 3 *P2 tbl, p1, p1 tbl, p1, p4 tbl, p2, k1, p2, p2 tbl; rep from * to end.
Row 4 *K1 tbl, k2tog, p1, k1, p1, ssk, [k3 tbl, yo] twice, k2 tbl; rep from * to end.
Row 5 *P2 tbl, [p1, p3 tbl] twice, p2, k1, p2, p1 tbl; rep from * to end.

Row 6 *K2tog, p1, k1, p1, ssk, k2 tbl, yo, k5 tbl, yo, k2 tbl; rep from * to end.
Row 7 *P2 tbl, p1, p2 tbl, k1, p2 tbl, p1, p7 tbl; rep from * to end.
Row 8 *K2 tbl, yo, k1 tbl, yo, k4 tbl, k2tog, p1, k1, p1, ssk, k2 tbl; rep from * to end.
Row 9 *P2 tbl, p2, k1, p2, p4 tbl, p1, p1 tbl, p1, p2 tbl; rep from * to end.
Row 10 *K2 tbl, [yo, k3 tbl] twice, k2tog, p1, k1, p1, ssk, k1 tbl; rep from * to end.
Row 11 *P1 tbl, p2, k1, p2, [p3 tbl, p1] twice, p2 tbl; rep from * to end.
Row 12 *K2 tbl, yo, k5 tbl, yo, k2 tbl, k2tog, p1, k1, p1, ssk; rep from * to end.
Rep rows 1–12.

16-st rep

Stitch Key

☐ K on RS, p on WS

⊟ P on RS, k on WS

◯ Yo

⟋ K2tog

⟍ Ssk

Ⴓ K1 tbl on RS, p1 tbl on WS

▨ No stitch

allover

(multiple of 11 sts plus 1)
Rows 1 and 3 (RS) *P1, k10; rep from *, end p1.
Row 2 and all WS rows K1, *p10, k1; rep from * to end.
Rows 5, 9 and 13 *P1, [k1, yo] 3 times, k1, [ssk] 3 times; rep from *, end p1.
Rows 7 and 11 *P1, k2, [yo, k1] twice, yo, [ssk] 3 times; rep from *, end p1.

Rows 15 and 17 Rep row 1.
Rows 19, 23 and 27 *P1, [k2tog] 3 times, [k1, yo] 3 times, k1; rep from *, end p1.
Rows 21 and 25 *P1, [k2tog] 3 times, [yo, k1] twice, yo, k2; rep from *, end p1.
Row 28 Rep row 2.
Rep rows 1–28.

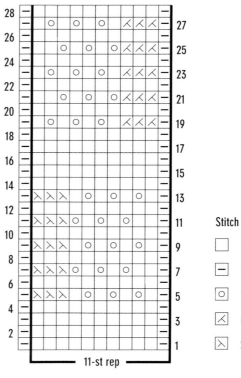

Stitch Key

☐ K on RS, p on WS

— P on RS, k on WS

⊙ Yo

⟋ K2tog

⟍ Ssk

11-st rep

(multiple of 22 sts plus 1)

Row 1 (RS) Ssk, *[yo, ssk] twice, k3, [k2tog, yo] twice, S2KP, yo, ssk, yo, [(k1, yo) 3 times, k1] in next st, yo, k2tog, yo, S2KP; rep from *, end last rep k2tog (instead of S2KP).

Row 2 and all WS rows Purl.

Row 3 Ssk, *[yo, ssk] twice, k1, [k2tog, yo] twice, S2KP, yo, ssk, yo, k7, yo, k2tog, yo, S2KP; rep from *, end last rep k2tog.

Row 5 Ssk, *yo, ssk, yo, S2KP, yo, k2tog, yo, S2KP, yo, ssk, yo, k7, yo, k2tog, yo, S2KP; rep from *, end last rep k2tog.

Row 7 Ssk, *yo, ssk, yo, [(k1, yo) 3 times, k1] in next st, yo, k2tog, yo, S2KP, [yo, ssk] twice, k3, [k2tog, yo] twice, S2KP; rep from *, end last rep k2tog.

Row 9 Ssk, *yo, ssk, yo, k7, yo, k2tog, yo, S2KP, [yo, ssk] twice, k1, [k2tog, yo] twice, S2KP; rep from *, end last rep k2tog.

Row 11 Ssk, *yo, ssk, yo, k7, yo, k2tog, yo, S2KP, yo, ssk, yo, S2KP, yo, k2tog, yo, S2KP; rep from *, end last rep k2tog.

Row 12 Purl.

Rep rows 1–12.

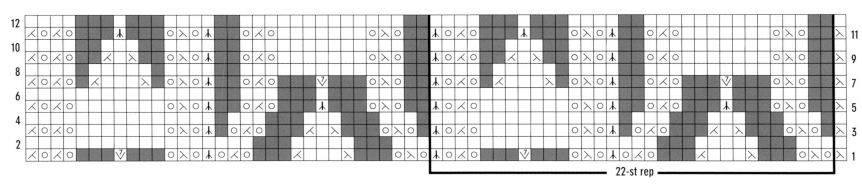

— 22-st rep —

Stitch Key

☐	K on RS, p on WS
⊙	Yo
╱	K2tog
╲	Ssk
⅄	S2KP
⊽	[(K1, yo) 3 times, k1] in a st
■	No stitch

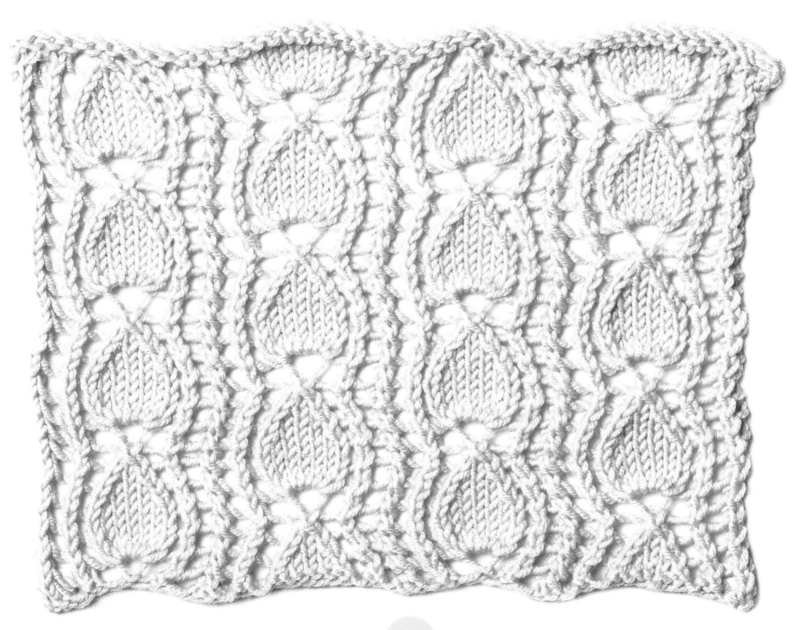

109 june bugs

(multiple of 12 sts plus 1)
Rows 1, 3 and 5 (RS) K2tog, *k2, yo, ssk, yo, k1, yo, k2tog, yo, k2, SK2P; rep from *, end last rep ssk (instead of SK2P).
Row 2 and all WS rows Purl.
Row 7 K2tog, *k1, yo, k2tog, yo, k3, yo, ssk, yo, k1, SK2P; rep from *, end last rep ssk.
Row 9 K2tog, *yo, k2tog, yo, k5, yo, ssk, yo, SK2P; rep from *, end last rep ssk.
Rows 11, 13 and 15 K1, *yo, k2tog, yo, k2, SK2P, k2, yo, ssk, yo, k1; rep from * to end.
Row 17 K1, *k1, yo, ssk, yo, k1, SK2P, k1, yo, k2tog, yo, k2; rep from * to end.
Row 19 K1, *k2, yo, ssk, yo, SK2P, yo, k2tog, yo, k3; rep from * to end.
Row 20 Purl.
Rep rows 1–20.

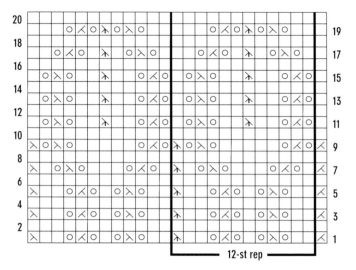

12-st rep

Stitch Key

☐	K on RS, p on WS
⊙	Yo
╱	K2tog
╲	Ssk
⅄	SK2P

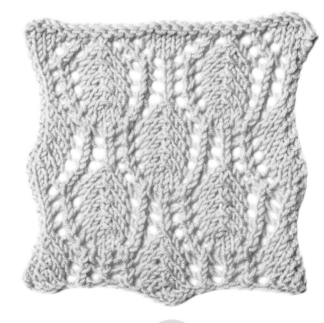

110 medallions

8-st Cable Sl 1 st to cn and hold to *front*, sl next 6 sts to 2nd cn and hold to *back*, k1 from LH needle, then [p1, k4, p1] from 2nd cn, then k1 from first cn.
(multiple of 18 sts plus 10)
Row 1 (RS) *P1, k1, p1, k2tog, yo twice, ssk, p1, k1; rep from *, end p1.
Row 2 *[K1, p1] twice, [p1, p1 tbl] into double yo, p1, k1, p1; rep from *, end k1.
Row 3 *P1, k1, p1, yo, k2tog, ssk, yo, p1, k1; rep from *, end p1.
Row 4 *K1, p1, k1, p4, k1, p1; rep from *, end k1.
Rows 5 and 6 Rep rows 1 and 2.
Row 7 *P1, k1, p1, yo, k2tog, ssk, yo, p1, k1, p1, 8-st Cable; rep from * to last 10 sts, end p1, k1, p1, yo, k2tog, ssk, yo, p1, k1, p1.
Row 8 Rep row 4.
Rows 9–14 Rep rows 1–6.
Row 15 *P1, 8-st Cable, p1, k1, p1, yo, k2tog, ssk, yo, p1, k1; rep from * to last 10 sts, p1, 8-st Cable, p1.
Row 16 Rep row 4.
Rep rows 1–16.

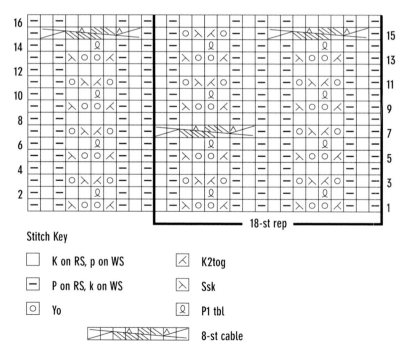

18-st rep

Stitch Key

☐	K on RS, p on WS	╱	K2tog
—	P on RS, k on WS	╲	Ssk
⊙	Yo	Ω	P1 tbl
			8-st cable

(multiple of 15 sts plus 2)
Row 1 (RS) *P2, k9, k3tog, yo, k1, yo; rep from *, end p2.
Row 2 and all WS rows K2, *p13, k2; rep from * to end.
Row 3 *P2, k7, k3tog, [k1, yo] twice, k1; rep from *, end p2.
Row 5 *P2, k5, k3tog, k2, yo, k1, yo, k2; rep from *, end p2.
Row 7 *P2, k3, k3tog, k3, yo, k1, yo, k3; rep from *, end p2.
Row 9 *P2, yo, k1, yo, SK2P, k9; rep from *, end p2.
Row 11 *P2, [k1, yo] twice, k1, SK2P, k7; rep from *, end p2.
Row 13 *P2, k2, yo, k1, yo, k2, SK2P, k5; rep from *, end p2.
Row 15 *P2, k3, yo, k1, yo, k3, SK2P, k3; rep from *, end p2.
Row 16 Rep row 2.
Rep rows 1–16.

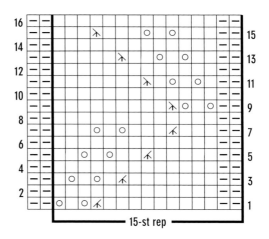

15-st rep

Stitch Key

☐ K on RS, p on WS

— P on RS, k on WS

◎ Yo

⼂ K3tog

⽊ SK2P

allover

(multiple of 15 sts plus 4)

Row 1 (RS) Ssk, yo, *k3tog, k1, [yo, k1 tbl] 3 times, yo, k1, [ssk] twice, k3; rep from *, end yo, k2tog.
Row 2 and all WS rows Purl.
Row 3 Ssk, yo, *ssk, k2, yo, k3, yo, k1 tbl, yo, k1, [ssk] twice, k2; rep from *, end yo, k2tog.
Row 5 Ssk, yo, *ssk, k1, yo, k5, yo, k1 tbl, yo, k1, [ssk] twice, k1; rep from *, end yo, k2tog.
Row 7 Ssk, yo, *ssk, yo, k3, k2tog, k1, [yo, k1 tbl] twice, yo, k1, [ssk] twice; rep from *, end yo, k2tog.
Row 9 Ssk, yo, *k3, [k2tog] twice, k1, [yo, k1 tbl] 3 times, yo, k1, sssk; rep from *, end yo, k2tog.
Row 11 Ssk, yo, *k2, [k2tog] twice, k1, yo, k1 tbl, yo, k3, yo, k2, k2tog; rep from *, end yo, k2tog.
Row 13 Ssk, yo, *k1, [k2tog] twice, k1, yo, k1 tbl, yo, k5, yo, k1, k2tog; rep from *, end yo, k2tog.
Row 15 Ssk, yo, *[k2tog] twice, k1, [yo, k1 tbl] twice, yo, k1, ssk, k3, yo, k2tog; rep from *, end yo, k2tog.
Row 16 Purl.

Rep rows 1–16.

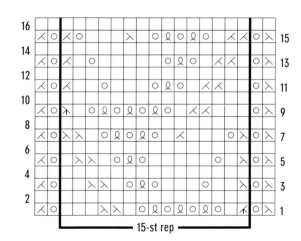

Stitch Key

☐	K on RS, p on WS
⊙	Yo
ℓ	K1 tbl
⟋	K2tog
⟍	Ssk
⟋	K3tog
⟍	Sssk

Make Bobble (MB) K into front, back and front of next st, turn, p3, turn, S2KP.

(multiple of 18 sts plus 1)

Row 1 (RS) *P1, ssk, k4, p2, yo, k1, yo, p2, k4, k2tog; rep from *, end p1.

Row 2 *K1, p5, k2, p3, k2, p5; rep from *, end k1.

Row 3 *P1, ssk, k3, p2, yo, k3, yo, p2, k3, k2tog; rep from *, end p1.

Row 4 *K1, p4, k2, p5, k2, p4; rep from *, end k1.

Row 5 *P1, ssk, k2, p2, yo, k2, MB, k2, yo, p2, k2, k2tog; rep from *, end p1.

Row 6 *K1, p3, k2, p7, k2, p3; rep from *, end k1.

Row 7 *P1, ssk, k1, p2, yo, ssk, k3, k2tog, yo, p2, k1, k2tog; rep from *, end p1.

Row 8 *K1, p2, k2, p7, k2, p2; rep from *, end k1.

Row 9 *P1, ssk, p2, yo, k1, yo, ssk, k1, k2tog, yo, k1, yo, p2, k2tog; rep from *, end p1.

Row 10 *K1, p1, k2, p9, k2, p1; rep from *, end k1.

Row 11 *P1, ssk, p1, yo, k3, yo, S2KP, yo, k3, yo, p1, k2tog; rep from *, end p1.

Row 12 *K1, p1, k1, p11, k1, p1; rep from *, end k1.

Row 13 *P1, ssk, yo, k2, MB, k2, yo, k1, yo, k2, MB, k2, yo, k2tog; rep from *, end p1.

Row 14 *K1, p17; rep from *, end k1.

Row 15 K2tog, *yo, ssk, k3, k2tog, yo, k1, yo, ssk, k3, k2tog, yo, S2KP; rep from *, end last rep ssk (instead of S2KP).

Rows 16, 18 and 20 Purl.

Row 17 *[K1, yo] twice, ssk, k1, k2tog, yo, k3, yo, ssk, k1, k2tog, yo, k1, yo; rep from *, end k1.

Row 19 K4, *yo, S2KP, yo, k5, yo, S2KP, yo, k7; rep from *, end last rep k4 (instead of k7).

Row 21 *K1, yo, p2, k4, k2tog, p1, ssk, k4, p2, yo; rep from *, end k1.

Row 22 *P2, k2, p5, k1, p5, k2, p1; rep from *, end p1.

Row 23 *K2, yo, p2, k3, k2tog, p1, ssk, k3, p2, yo, k1; rep from *, end k1.

Row 24 *P3, k2, p4, k1, p4, k2, p2; rep from *, end p1.

Row 25 K1, *k2, yo, p2, k2, k2tog, p1, ssk, k2, p2, yo, k2, MB; rep from *, end last rep k1 (instead of MB).

Row 26 *P4, k2, p3, k1, p3, k2, p3; rep from *, end p1.

Row 27 *K2, k2tog, yo, p2, k1, k2tog, p1, ssk, k1, p2, yo, ssk, k1; rep from *, end k1.

Row 28 *P4, k2, p2, k1, p2, k2, p3; rep from *, end p1.

Row 29 *K1, k2tog, yo, k1, yo, p2, k2tog, p1, ssk, p2, yo, k1, yo, ssk; rep from *, end k1.

Row 30 *P5, k2, p1, k1, p1, k2, p4; rep from *, end p1.

Row 31 K2tog, *yo, k3, yo, p1, k2tog, p1, ssk, p1, yo, k3, yo, S2KP; rep from *, end last rep ssk (instead of S2KP).

Row 32 P6, *[k1, p1] twice, k1, p11; rep from *, end last rep p6 (instead of p11).

Row 33 *K1, yo, k2, MB, k2, yo, k2tog, p1, ssk, yo, k2, MB, k2, yo; rep from *, end k1.

Row 34 P9, *k1, p17; rep from *, end last rep p9 (instead of p17).
Row 35 *K1, yo, ssk, k3, k2tog, yo, S2KP, yo, ssk, k3, k2tog, yo; rep from *, end k1.
Rows 36 and 38 Purl.
Row 37 *K2, yo, ssk, k1, k2tog, yo, [k1, yo] 3 times, ssk, k1, k2tog, yo, k1; rep from *, end k1.
Row 39 K3, *yo, S2KP, yo, k7, yo, S2KP, yo, k5; rep from *, end last rep k3 (instead of k5).
Row 40 Purl.
Rep rows 1–40.

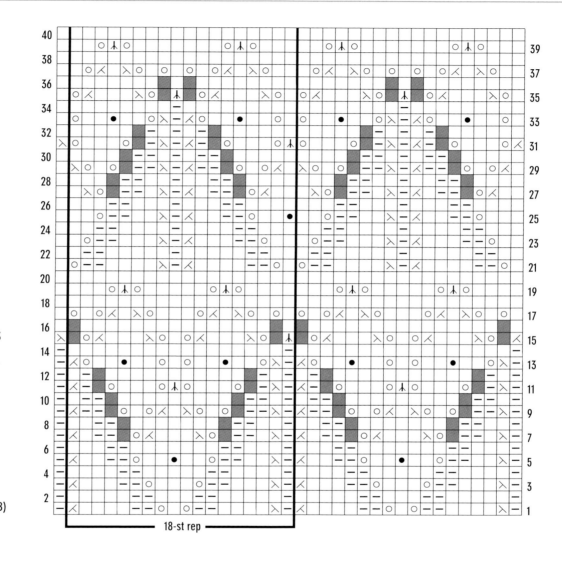

18-st rep

Stitch Key

	K on RS, p on WS
—	P on RS, k on WS
○	Yo
╱	K2tog
╲	Ssk
⅄	S2KP
▩	No stitch
●	Make Bobble (MB)

(multiple of 18 sts plus 1)

Row 1 (RS) K1, *k1, p1, ssk, [k3, yo] twice, k3, k2tog, p1, k2; rep from * to end.

Row 2 and all WS rows P the purl sts and yos, and k the knit sts.

Row 3 K1, *k2, p1, ssk, k1, yo, k5, yo, k1, k2tog, p1, k3; rep from * to end.

Row 5 P1, *ssk, k1, p1, k1, yo, k2, yo, S2KP, yo, k2, yo, k1, p1, k1, k2tog, p1; rep from * to end.

Row 7 K1, *p1, ssk, k1, yo, k2, yo, k1, S2KP, k1, yo, k2, yo, k1, k2tog, p1, k1; rep from * to end.

Rows 9, 11 and 13 K1, *p1, ssk, [yo, k2] twice, S2KP, [k2, yo] twice, k2tog, p1, k1; rep from * to end.

Row 15 K2, *ssk, yo, k1, yo, k2, k2tog, p1, ssk, k2, yo, k1, yo, k2tog, yo, S2KP, yo; rep from * to last 17 sts, end ssk, yo, k1, yo, k2, k2tog, p1, ssk, k2, yo, k1, yo, k2tog, k2.

Row 17 K2, *k2, yo, k2, k2tog, p1, k1, p1, ssk, [k2, yo] twice, S2KP, yo; rep from * to last 17 sts, end k2, yo, k2, k2tog, p1, k1, p1, ssk, k2, yo, k4.

Row 19 K1, *k1, yo, k3, k2tog, p1, k3, p1, ssk, k3, yo, k2; rep from * to end.

Row 21 K1, *k2, yo, k1, k2tog, p1, k5, p1, ssk, k1, yo, k3; rep from * to end.

Row 23 Ssk, yo, *k2, yo, k1, p1, k1, k2tog, p1, ssk,
k1, p1, k1, yo, k2, yo, S2KP, yo; rep from * to last 17
sts, end k2, yo, k1, p1, k1, k2tog, p1, ssk, k1, p1, k1,
yo, k2, yo, k2tog.
Row 25 Ssk, *k1, yo, k2, yo, k1, k2tog, p1, k1, p1,
ssk, k1, yo, k2, yo, k1, S2KP; rep from * to last 17
sts, end k1, yo, k2, yo, k1, k2tog, p1, k1, p1, ssk, k1,
yo, k2, yo, k1, k2tog.
Rows 27, 29 and 31 Ssk, *[k2, yo] twice, k2tog, p1,
k1, p1, ssk, [yo, k2] twice, S2KP; rep from * to last
17 sts, end [k2, yo] twice, k2tog, p1, k1, p1, ssk, [yo,
k2] twice, k2tog.
Row 33 P1, *ssk, k2, yo, k1, yo, k2tog, yo, S2KP, yo,
ssk, yo, k1, yo, k2, k2tog, p1; rep from * to end.
Row 35 K1, *p1, ssk, [k2, yo] twice, S2KP, [yo, k2]
twice, k2tog, p1, k1; rep from * to end.
Row 36 Rep row 2.
Rep rows 1–36.

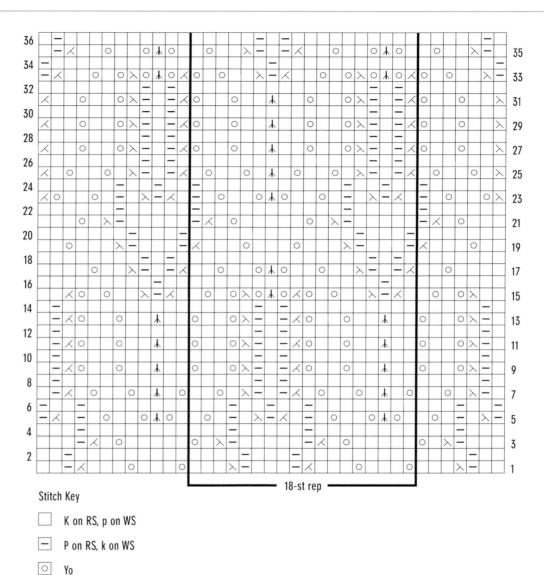

18-st rep

Stitch Key

☐ K on RS, p on WS

☐ (−) P on RS, k on WS

☐ (○) Yo

☐ (╱) K2tog

☐ (╲) Ssk

☐ (人) S2KP

(multiple of 34 sts plus 2)

Row 1 (RS) K1, *yo, ssk, k2, yo, ssk, p2, yo, k4, ssk, k6, k2tog, k4, yo, p2, k2, yo, ssk, k2; rep from *, end k1.

Row 2 K1, *yo, p2tog, p2, yo, p2tog, k2, p1, yo, p4, p2tog, p4, ssp, p4, yo, p1, k2, p2, yo, p2tog, p2; rep from *, end k1.

Row 3 K1, *yo, ssk, k2, yo, ssk, p2, k2, yo, k4, ssk, k2, k2tog, k4, yo, k2, p2, k2, yo, ssk, k2; rep from *, end k1.

Row 4 K1, *yo, p2tog, p2, yo, p2tog, k2, p3, yo, p4, p2tog, ssp, p4, yo, p3, k2, p2, yo, p2tog, p2; rep from *, end k1.

Rows 5–12 Rep rows 1–4 twice.

Row 13 K1, *k3, k2tog, k4, yo, p2, [k2, yo, ssk] 3 times, p2, yo, k4, ssk, k3; rep from *, end k1.

Row 14 K1, *p2, ssp, p4, yo, p1, k2, [p2, yo, p2tog] 3 times, k2, p1, yo, p4, p2tog, p2; rep from *, end k1.

Row 15 K1, *k1, k2tog, k4, yo, k2, p2, [k2, yo, ssk] 3 times, p2, k2, yo, k4, ssk, k1; rep from *, end k1.

Row 16 K1, *ssp, p4, yo, p3, k2, [p2, yo, p2tog] 3 times, k2, p3, yo, p4, p2tog; rep from *, end k1.

Rows 17–24 Rep rows 13–16 twice.

Rep rows 1–24.

Stitch Key

☐	K on RS, p on WS
─	P on RS, k on WS
☉	Yo
⟋	K2tog on RS, p2tog on WS
⟍	Ssk on RS, ssp on WS

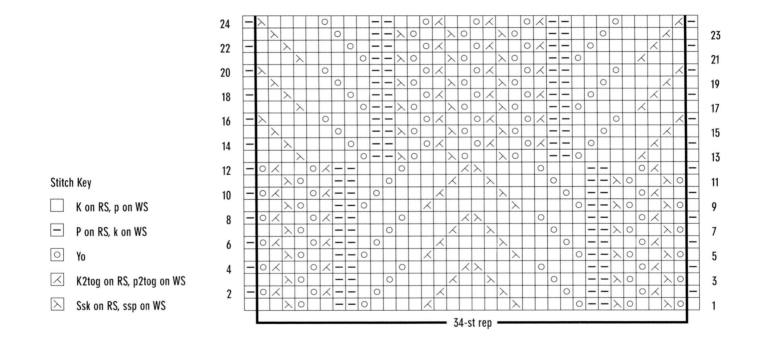

34-st rep

(multiple of 17 sts plus 1)

Row 1 (RS) *P1, k16; rep from *, end p1.

Row 2 K1, *p16, k1; rep from * to end.

Row 3 *P1, yo, k3, ssk, k6, k2tog, k3, yo; rep from *, end p1.

Row 4 K1, *p1, yo, p3, p2tog, p4, ssp, p3, yo, p1, k1; rep from * to end.

Row 5 *P1, k2, yo, k3, ssk, k2, k2tog, k3, yo, k2; rep from *, end p1.

Row 6 K1, *p3, yo, p3, p2tog, ssp, p3, yo, p3, k1; rep from * to end.

Rows 7–14 Rep rows 3–6 twice more.

Rows 15 and 17 Rep row 1.

Row 16 Rep row 2.

Rows 18 and 20 Knit.

Row 19 *P1, [yo, ssk] 4 times, [k2tog, yo] 4 times; rep from *, end p1.

Rows 21 and 22 Rep rows 1 and 2.

Row 23 *P1, [yo, k1] twice, yo, [ssk] 3 times, [k2tog] 3 times, [yo, k1] twice, yo; rep from *, end p1.

Row 24 Rep row 2.

Row 25 Rep row 1.

Rows 26–28 Rep rows 18–20.

Rep rows 1–28.

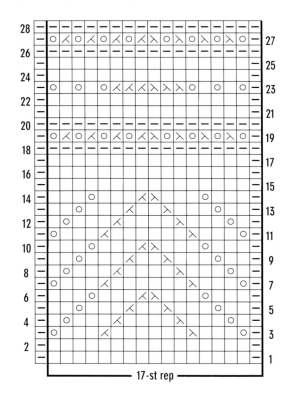

Stitch Key

□	K on RS, p on WS
−	P on RS, k on WS
⊙	Yo
⟋	K2tog on RS, p2tog on WS
⟍	Ssk on RS, ssp on WS

allover

(multiple of 8 sts plus 1)
Row 1 (RS) *K2, yo, ssk, k1, k2tog, yo, k1; rep from *, end k1.
Rows 2, 4 and 6 Purl.
Row 3 *K1, yo, ssk, yo, S2KP, yo, k2tog, yo; rep from *, end k1.
Rows 5 and 7 *K1, yo, S2KP, yo; rep from *, end k1.
Row 8 Purl.
Rep rows 1–8.

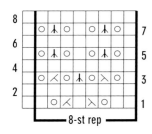

K on RS, p on WS

Yo

K2tog

Ssk

S2KP

8-st rep

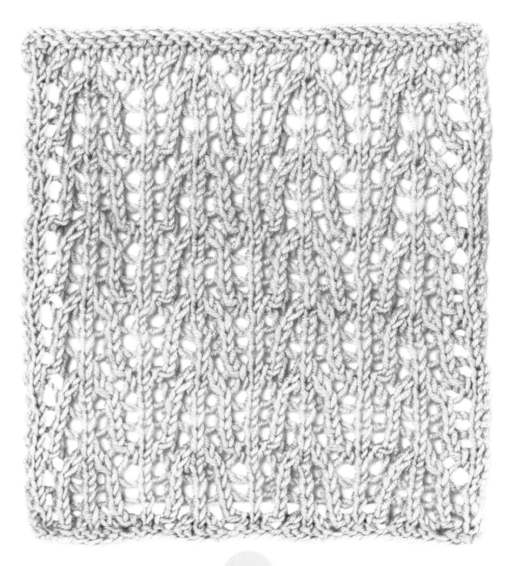

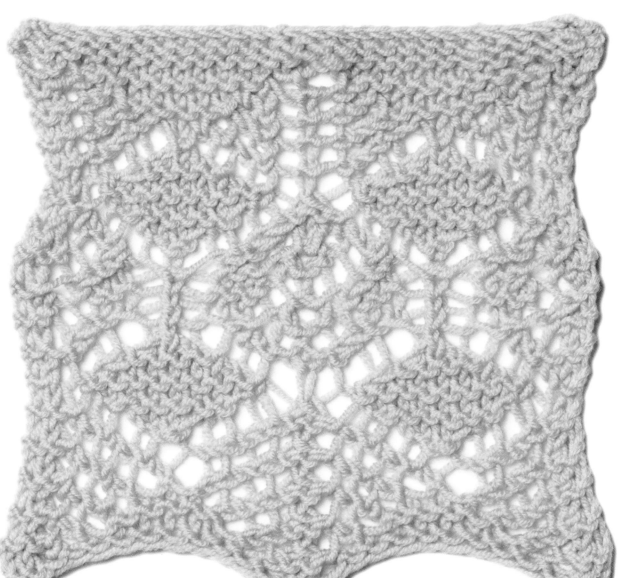

(multiple of 12 sts plus 3)

Note For ease of working, mark RS of work.

Row 1 (RS) K1, k2tog, yo, k9, *yo, SK2P, yo, k9; rep from *, end yo, k2tog, k1.

Row 2 K2, *k2tog, yo, k7, yo, k2tog, k1; rep from * to last st, k1.

Row 3 K1, [k2tog, yo] twice, k5, *yo, k2tog, yo, SK2P, yo, k2tog, yo, k5; rep from * to last 5 sts, end [yo, k2tog] twice, k1.

Row 4 K2, *[k2tog, yo] twice, k3, [yo, k2tog] twice, k1; rep from * to last st, k1.

Row 5 K1, [k2tog, yo] 3 times, *k1, [yo, k2tog] twice, yo, SK2P, yo, [k2tog, yo] twice; rep from * to last 8 sts, end k1, [yo, k2tog] 3 times, k1.

Row 6 K2, *[k2tog, yo] 3 times, k1, [yo, k2tog] twice, k1; rep from * to last st, k1.

Row 7 Rep row 5.

Row 8 Rep row 4.

Row 9 Rep row 3.

Row 10 Rep row 2.

Row 11 Rep row 1.

Row 12 K2, *yo, k2tog, k7, k2tog, yo, k1; rep from * to last st, k1.

Row 13 K3, *yo, k2tog, k5, k2tog, yo, k3; rep from * to end.

Row 14 K3, *k1, yo, k2tog, k3, k2tog, yo, k4; rep from * to end.

Row 15 K2, *[yo, k2tog, k1] twice, [k2tog, yo, k1] twice; rep from * to last st, k1.

Row 16 K3, *yo, k2tog, k1, yo, SK2P, yo, k1, k2tog, yo, k3; rep from * to end.

Row 17 K2, k2tog, yo, k2, *yo, SK2P, yo, k2, yo, k2tog, yo, SK2P, yo, k2; rep from * to last 9 sts, end yo, SK2P, yo, k2, yo, k2tog, k2.

Row 18 K1, k2tog, yo, k3, *yo, SK2P, yo, k3; rep from * to last 3 sts, end yo, k2tog, k1.

Row 19 K2, *yo, k2tog, k2, yo, SK2P, yo, k2, k2tog, yo, k1; rep from * to last st, k1.

Row 20 Rep row 16.

Row 21 K2, [k2tog, yo, k1] twice, *yo, k2tog, k1, yo, k2tog, yo, SK2P, yo, k1, k2tog, yo, k1; rep from * to last 7 sts, end [yo, k2tog, k1] twice, k1.

Row 22 [K1, k2tog, yo] twice, k3, *yo, k2tog, k1, yo, SK2P, yo, k1, k2tog,yo, k3; rep from * to last 6 sts, end [yo, k2tog, k1] twice.

Row 23 K3, *k2tog, yo, k5, yo, k2tog, k3; rep from * to end.

Row 24 Rep row 2.

Row 25 Rep row 1.

Row 26 Rep row 12.

Row 27 Rep row 13.

Row 28 K1, *k1, [yo, k2tog] twice, k3, [k2tog, yo] twice; rep from *, end k2.

Row 29 K3, *[yo, k2tog] twice, k1, [k2tog, yo] twice, k3; rep from * to end.

Row 30 K1, *k1, [yo, k2tog] twice, yo, SK2P, yo, [k2tog, yo] twice; rep from *, end k2.

Row 31 Rep row 29.

Row 32 Rep row 28.

Row 33 Rep row 13.

Row 34 Rep row 12.

Row 35 K1, yo, k2tog, k9, *k2tog, yo, k10; rep from *, end k2tog, yo, k1.

Row 36 Knit.

Rep rows 1–36.

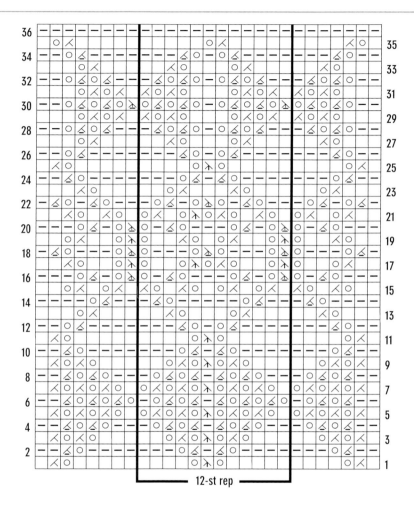

12-st rep

Stitch Key

☐ K on RS

▭ K on WS

○ Yo

◿ K2tog on RS

◺ K2tog on WS

↗ SK2P on RS

⬦ SK2P on WS

(multiple of 24 sts plus 1)

Row 1 (RS) P1, *yo, [k1, p1] twice, ssk, p1, k1, p2, k1, p1, k1, p2, k1, p1, k2tog, [p1, k1] twice, yo, p1; rep from * to end.

Row 2 *K1, p1, yo, [p1, k1] twice, p2tog, p1, k2, p1, k1, p1, k2, p1, ssp, [k1, p1] twice, yo, p1; rep from *, end k1.

Row 3 P1, *k1, p1, yo, [k1, p1] twice, ssk, p2, k1, p1, k1, p2, k2tog, [p1, k1] twice, yo, p1, k1, p1; rep from * to end.

Row 4 *[K1, p1] twice, yo, [p1, k1] twice, p2tog, [k1, p1] twice, k1, ssp, [k1, p1] twice, yo, p1, k1, p1; rep from *, end k1.

Row 5 P1, *[k1, p1] twice, yo, [k1, p1] twice, ssk, k1, p1, k1, k2tog, [p1, k1] twice, yo, [p1, k1] twice, p1; rep from * to end.

Row 6 *[K1, p1] 3 times, yo, [p1, k1] twice, p2tog, k1, ssp, [k1, p1] twice, yo, [p1, k1] twice, p1; rep from *, end k1.

Row 7 P1, *yo, [k1, p1] twice, ssk, [k1, p1] 5 times, k1, k2tog, [p1, k1] twice, yo, p1; rep from * to end.

Row 8 *K1, p1, yo, [p1, k1] twice, p2tog, [k1, p1] 4 times, k1, ssp, [k1, p1] twice, yo, p1; rep from *, end k1.

Row 9 P1, *k1, p1, yo, [k1, p1] twice, ssk, [k1, p1] 3 times, k1, k2tog, [p1, k1] twice, yo, p1, k1, p1; rep from * to end.

Rows 10–12 Rep rows 4–6.

Row 13 P1, *[k1, p1] twice, k1, k2tog, [p1, k1] twice, yo, p1, yo, [k1, p1] twice, ssk, [k1, p1] 3 times; rep from * to end.

Row 14 *[K1, p1] twice, k1, ssp, [k1, p1] twice, yo, p1, k1, p1, yo, [p1, k1] twice, p2tog, [k1, p1] twice; rep from *, end k1.

Row 15 P1, *k1, p1, k1, k2tog, [p1, k1] twice, yo, [p1, k1] twice, p1, yo, [k1, p1] twice, ssk, [k1, p1] twice; rep from * to end.

Row 16 *K1, p1, k1, ssp, [k1, p1] twice, yo, [p1, k1] 3 times, p1, yo, [p1, k1] twice, p2tog, k1, p1; rep from *, end k1.

Row 17 P1, *k1, k2tog, [p1, k1] twice, yo, [p1, k1] 4 times, p1, yo, [k1, p1] twice, ssk, k1, p1; rep from * to end.

Row 18 *K1, ssp, [k1, p1] twice, yo, [p1, k1] 5 times, p1, yo, [p1, k1] twice, p2tog; rep from *, end k1.

Row 19 Rep row 13.

Row 20 *K1, p1, k3, ssp, [k1, p1] twice, yo, p1, k1, p1, yo, [p1, k1] twice, p2tog, k3, p1; rep from *, end k1.

Row 21 P1, *k1, p2, k2tog, [p1, k1] twice, yo, [p1, k1] twice, p1, yo, [k1, p1] twice, ssk, p2, k1, p1; rep from * to end.

Rows 22–24 Rep rows 16–18.

Rep rows 1–24.

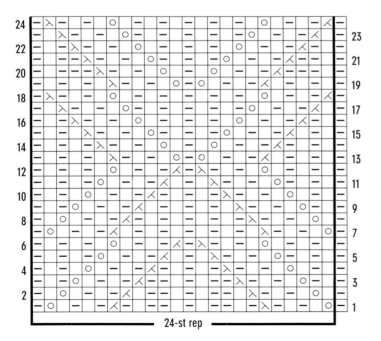

Stitch Key

	K on RS, p on WS
−	P on RS, k on WS
○	Yo
⟋	K2tog on RS, p2tog on WS
⟍	Ssk on RS, ssp on WS

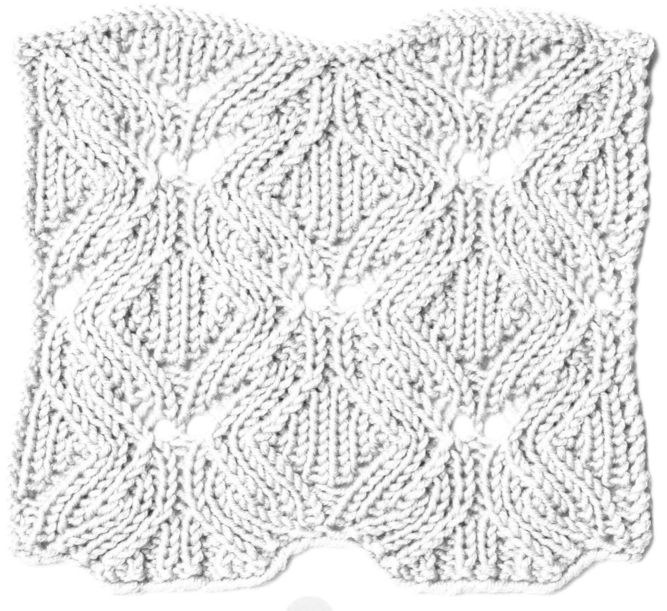

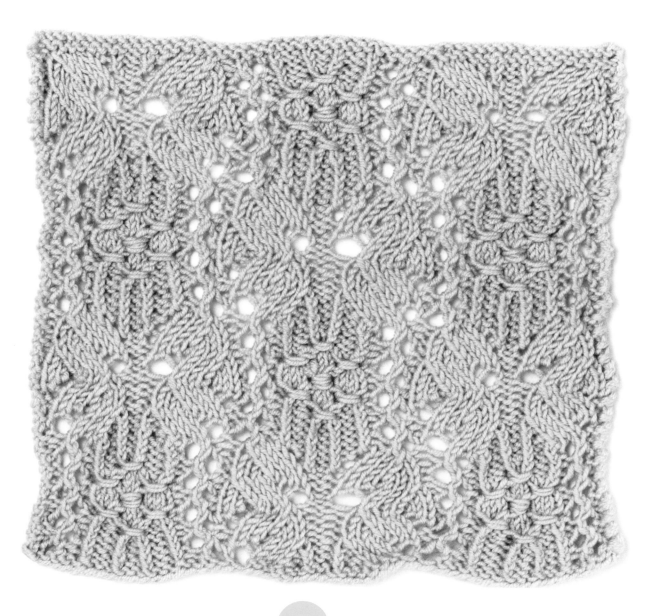

Wrap 4 sts twice K4, then sl these 4 sts to a cn, wrap yarn around sts counterclockwise twice, then leaving yarn at back, return sts to RH needle.

Wrap 4 sts 5 times Work as above, wrapping yarn 5 times.

(multiple of 34 sts plus 2)

(**Note** For a symmetrical pattern, work the first 18 sts of the repeat once more before working the last selvage st.)

Row 1 (RS) K1, *p1, yo, ssk, p1, k1, [p2, k1 tbl] twice, p2, k1, p1, k2tog, yo, p1, yo, k2, ssk, [p2, k1 tbl] twice, p2, k2tog, k2, yo; rep from *, end k1.

Row 2 K1, *p1, yo, p2, p2tog, k1, p1 tbl, k2, p1 tbl, k1, ssp, p2, yo, p1, k1, p2, k1, p1 tbl, [k2, p1 tbl] 3 times, k1, p2, k1; rep from *, end k1.

Row 3 K1, *p1, k2tog, yo, p1, k1 tbl, [p2, k1 tbl] 3 times, p1, yo, ssk, p1, k2, yo, k2, ssk, k1 tbl, p2, k1 tbl, k2tog, k2, yo, k2; rep from *, end k1.

Row 4 K1, *p3, yo, p2, p2tog, k2, ssp, p2, yo, p3, k1, p2, k1, p1 tbl, [k2, p1 tbl] 3 times, k1, p2, k1; rep from *, end k1.

Row 5 K1, *p1, yo, ssk, p1, k1 tbl, p2, Wrap 4 sts twice, p2, k1 tbl, p1, k2tog, yo, p1, yo, k2, ssk, k3, p2, k3, k2tog, k2, yo; rep from *, end k1.

Row 6 K1, *p1, yo, p2, p2tog, p2, k2, p2, ssp, p2, yo, p1, k1, p2, k1, p1 tbl, k2, p4, k2, p1 tbl, k1, p2, k1; rep from *, end k1.

Row 7 K1, *p1, k2tog, yo, p1, Wrap 4 sts twice, k2, Wrap 4 sts twice, p1, yo, ssk, p1, k2, yo, k2, ssk, k1, p2, k1, k2tog, k2, yo, k2; rep from *, end k1.

Row 8 K1, *p3, yo, p2, p2tog, k2, ssp, p2, yo, p3, k1, p2, k1, p10, k1, p2, k1; rep from *, end k1.

Row 9 K1, *p1, yo, ssk, p1, k3, Wrap 4 sts 5 times, k3, p1, k2tog, yo, p1, k3, k2tog, k2, yo, p2, yo, k2, ssk, k3; rep from *, end k1.

Row 10 K1, *p2, ssp, p2, yo, p1, k2, p1, yo, p2, p2tog, [p2, k1] twice, p10, k1, p2, k1; rep from *, end k1.

Row 11 K1, *p1, k2tog, yo, p1, Wrap 4 sts twice, k2, Wrap 4 sts twice, p1, yo, ssk, p1, k1, k2tog, k2, yo, k2, p2, k2, yo, k2, ssk, k1; rep from *, end k1.

Row 12 K1, *ssp, p2, yo, p3, k2, p3, yo, p2, p2tog, k1, p2, k1, p1, k2, p4, k2, p1, k1, p2, k1; rep from *, end k1.

Row 13 K1, *p1, yo, ssk, p1, k1 tbl, p2, Wrap 4 sts twice, p2, k1 tbl, p1, k2tog, yo, p1, k3, k2tog, k2, yo, p2, yo, k2, ssk, k3; rep from *, end k1.

Row 14 K1, *p2, ssp, p2, yo, p1, k2, p1, yo, p2, p2tog, [p2, k1] twice, p1 tbl, k2, [p1, k2] twice, p1 tbl, k1, p2, k1; rep from *, end k1.

Row 15 K1, *p1, k2tog, yo, p1, k1 tbl, [p2, k1 tbl] 3 times, p1, yo, ssk, p1, k1, k2tog, k2, yo, p1, k1 tbl, p2, k1 tbl, p1, yo, k2, ssk, k1; rep from *, end k1.

Row 16 K1, *ssp, p2, yo, [k2, p1 tbl] twice, k2, yo, p2, p2tog, k1, p2, k1, p1 tbl, [k2, p1 tbl] 3 times, k1, p2, k1; rep from *, end k1.

Row 17 K1, *p1, yo, k2, ssk, [p2, k1 tbl] twice, p2, k2tog, k2, yo, p1, yo, ssk, p1, k1, [p2, k1 tbl] twice, p2, k1, p1, k2tog, yo; rep from *, end k1.

Row 18 K1, *p2, k1, p1 tbl, [k2, p1 tbl] 3 times, k1, p2, k1, p1, yo, p2, p2tog, k1, p1 tbl, k2, p1 tbl, k1, ssp, p2, yo, p1, k1; rep from *, end k1.

Row 19 K1, *p1, k2, yo, k2, ssk, k1 tbl, p2, k1 tbl, k2tog, k2, yo, k2, p1, k2tog, yo, p1, k1 tbl, [p2, k1 tbl] 3 times, p1, yo, ssk; rep from *, end k1.

Row 20 K1, *p2, k1, p1 tbl, [k2, p1 tbl] 3 times, k1, p2, k1, p3, yo, p2, p2tog, k2, ssp, p2, yo, p3, k1; rep from *, end k1.

Row 21 K1, *p1, yo, k2, ssk, k3, p2, k3, k2tog, k2, yo, p1, yo, ssk, p1, k1 tbl, p2, Wrap 4 sts twice, p2, k1 tbl, p1, k2tog, yo; rep from *, end k1.

Row 22 K1, *p2, k1, p1 tbl, k2, p4, k2, p1 tbl, k1, p2, k1, p1, yo, p2, p2tog, p2, k2, p2, ssp, p2, yo, p1, k1; rep from *, end k1.

Row 23 K1, *p1, k2, yo, k2, ssk, k1, p2, k1, k2tog, k2, yo, k2, p1, k2tog, yo, p1, Wrap 4 sts twice, k2, Wrap 4 sts twice, p1, yo, ssk; rep from *, end k1.

Row 24 K1, *p2, k1, p10, k1, p2, k1, p3, yo, p2, p2tog, k2, ssp, p2, yo, p3, k1; rep from *, end k1.

Row 25 K1, *p1, k3, k2tog, k2, yo, p2, yo, k2, ssk, k3, p1, yo, ssk, p1, k3, Wrap 4 sts 5 times, k3, p1, k2tog, yo; rep from *, end k1.

Row 26 K1, *p2, k1, p10, [k1, p2] twice, ssp, p2, yo, p1, k2, p1, yo, p2, p2tog, p2, k1; rep from *, end k1.

Row 27 K1, *p1, k1, k2tog, k2, yo, k2, p2, k2, yo, k2, ssk, k1, p1, k2tog, yo, p1, Wrap 4 sts twice, k2, Wrap 4 sts twice, p1, yo, ssk; rep from *, end k1.

Row 28 K1, *p2, k1, p1, k2, p4, k2, p1, k1, p2, k1, ssp, p2, yo, p3, k2, p3, yo, p2, p2tog, k1; rep from *, end k1.

Row 29 K1, *p1, k3, k2tog, k2, yo, p2, yo, k2, ssk, k3, p1, yo, ssk, p1, k1 tbl, p2, Wrap 4 sts twice, p2, k1 tbl, p1, k2tog, yo; rep from *, end k1.

Row 30 K1, *p2, k1, p1 tbl, [k2, p1] twice, k2, p1 tbl, [k1, p2] twice, ssp, p2, yo, p1, k2, p1, yo, p2, p2tog, p2, k1; rep from *, end k1.

Row 31 K1, *p1, k1, k2tog, k2, yo, p1, k1 tbl, p2, k1 tbl, p1, yo, k2, ssk, k1, p1, k2tog, yo, p1, k1 tbl, [p2, k1 tbl] 3 times, p1, yo, ssk; rep from *, end k1.

Row 32 K1, *p2, k1, p1 tbl, [k2, p1 tbl] 3 times, k1, p2, k1, ssp, p2, yo, [k2, p1 tbl] twice, k2, yo, p2, p2tog, k1; rep from *, end k1.

Rep rows 1–32.

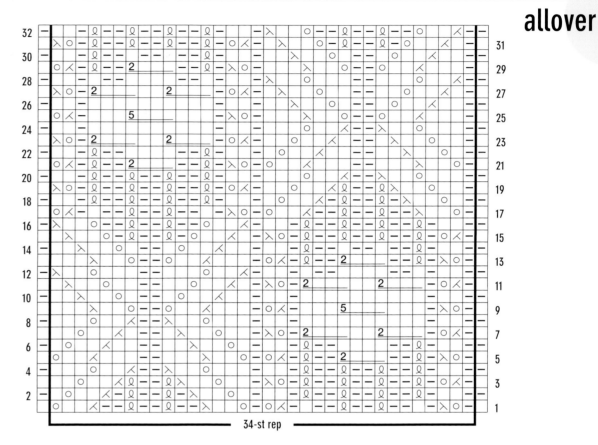

34-st rep

Stitch Key

☐	K on RS, p on WS	
─	P on RS, k on WS	
○	Yo	
⊼	K2tog on RS, p2tog on WS	
⋋	Ssk on RS, ssp on WS	
Ǫ	K1 tbl on RS, p1 tbl on WS	
2▭	Wrap 4 sts twice	
5▭	Wrap 4 sts 5 times	

121 loop-di-loop

Loop Stitch [K3, turn, p3, turn] 4 times, k3, do not turn.
(multiple of 6 sts plus 5)
Rows 1 and 3 (RS) Knit.
Row 2 and all WS rows Purl.

Row 5 K1, *work Loop St over 3 sts, k3; rep from *, end last rep k1 (instead of k3).
Rows 7 and 9 Knit.
Row 11 K1, *k3, work Loop St over 3 sts; rep from *, end k4.
Row 12 Purl.
Rep rows 1–12.

Stitch Key

☐ K on RS, p on WS

▭ Loop stitch

122 dewdrops

(multiple of 7 sts plus 2)
Row 1 (RS) K1, *k3, yo, SKP, k2; rep from *, end k1.
Row 2 K1, *p1, p2tog, yo, p1, yo, p2tog, p1; rep from *, end k1.
Row 3 K1, *SKP, yo, k3, yo, SKP; rep from *, end k1.
Row 4 Knit.
Row 5 K1, *k5, SKP, yo; rep from *, end k1.
Row 6 K1, *p1, yo, p2tog, p2, p2tog, yo; rep from *, end k1.
Row 7 K1, *k1, yo, [SKP] twice, yo, k2; rep from *, end k1.
Row 8 Knit.
Rep rows 1–8.

Stitch Key

☐ K on RS, p on WS

▬ K on WS

○ Yo

⤬ SKP

⤢ P2tog

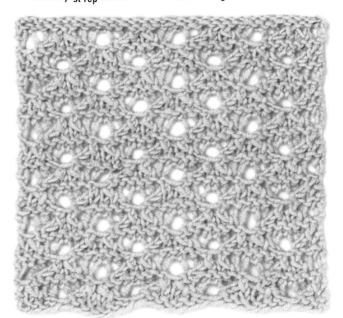

panels

123 diamond solitaire

(worked over 23 sts)
Row 1 (RS) K11, yo, ssk, k10.
Row 2 and all WS rows Purl.
Row 3 K9, k2tog, yo, k1, yo, ssk, k9.
Row 5 K8, k2tog, yo, k3, yo, ssk, k8.
Row 7 K7, k2tog, yo, k5, yo, ssk, k7.

Row 9 K6, k2tog, yo, k7, yo, ssk, k6.
Row 11 K5, k2tog, yo, k9, yo, ssk, k5.
Row 13 K4, k2tog, yo, k11, yo, ssk, k4.
Row 15 K3, k2tog, yo, k13, yo, ssk, k3.
Row 17 K2, k2tog, yo, k15, yo, ssk, k2.
Row 19 K1, k2tog, yo, k17, yo, ssk, k1.

Row 21 K2tog, yo, k19, yo, ssk.
Row 23 K2, yo, ssk, k15, k2tog, yo, k2.
Row 25 K3, yo, ssk, k13, k2tog, yo, k3.
Row 27 K4, yo, ssk, k11, k2tog, yo, k4.
Row 29 K5, yo, ssk, k9, k2tog, yo, k5.
Row 31 K6, yo, ssk, k7, k2tog, yo, k6.

Row 33 K7, yo, ssk, k5, k2tog, yo, k7.
Row 35 K8, yo, ssk, k3, k2tog, yo, k8.
Row 37 K9, yo, ssk, k1, k2tog, yo, k9.
Row 39 K10, yo, S2KP, yo, k10.
Row 40 Purl.
Rep rows 1–40.

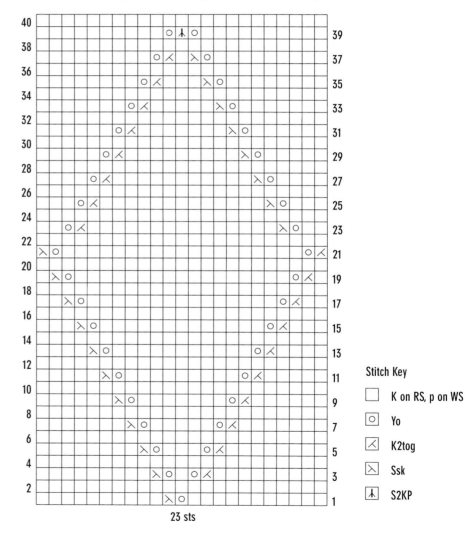

Stitch Key

	K on RS, p on WS
⊙	Yo
╱	K2tog
╲	Ssk
⋏	S2KP

23 sts

123

124 open hands

(worked over 23 sts)

Row 1 (RS) K8, k2tog, yo, k1, p1, k1, yo, ssk, k8.
Row 2 P7, ssp, p2, yo, k1, yo, p2, p2tog, p7.
Row 3 K6, k2tog, k1, yo, k2, p1, k2, yo, k1, ssk, k6.
Row 4 P5, ssp, p3, yo, p1, k1, p1, yo, p3, p2tog, p5.

Row 5 K4, k2tog, k2, yo, k3, p1, k3, yo, k2, ssk, k4.
Row 6 P3, ssp, p4, yo, p2, k1, p2, yo, p4, p2tog, p3.
Row 7 K2, k2tog, k3, yo, k4, p1, k4, yo, k3, ssk, k2.
Row 8 P1, ssp, p5, yo, p3, k1, p3, yo, p5, p2tog, p1.

Row 9 K2tog, k4, yo, k5, p1, k5, yo, k4, ssk.
Row 10 P11, k1, p11.
Row 11 K11, p1, k11.
Row 12 Rep row 10.
Rep rows 1–12.

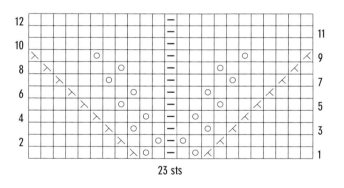

23 sts

Stitch Key

☐ K on RS, p on WS

— P on RS, k on WS

⦿ Yo

╱ K2tog on RS, p2tog on WS

╲ Ssk on RS, ssp on WS

125 climbing leaves

(worked over 24 sts)

Set-up row (WS) K4, p5, k4, p3, k8.

Row 1 (RS) P6, p2tog, k1, M1 purl, k2, p4, k2, yo, k1, yo, k2, p4—26 sts.

Row 2 K4, p7, k4, p2, k1, p1, k7.

Row 3 P5, p2tog, k1, M1 purl, p1, k2, p4, k3, yo, k1, yo, k3, p4—28 sts.

Row 4 K4, p9, k4, p2, k2, p1, k6.

Row 5 P4, p2tog, k1, p1, M1 purl, p1, k2, p4, ssk, k5, k2tog, p4—26 sts.

Row 6 K4, p7, k4, p2, k3, p1, k5.

Row 7 P3, p2tog, k1, p2, M1 purl, p1, k2, p4, ssk, k3, k2tog, p4—24 sts.

Row 8 K4, p5, k4, p2, k4, p1, k4.

Row 9 P4, yo, k1, yo, p4, k2, p4, ssk, k1, k2tog, p4.

Row 10 K4, p3, k4, p2, k4, p3, k4.

Row 11 P4, yo, k1, yo, k2, p4, k1, yo, k1, p2tog, p2, S2KP, p4.

Row 12 K8, p3, k4, p5, k4.

Row 13 P4, k2, yo, k1, yo, k2, p4, k2, M1 purl, k1, p2tog, p6—26 sts.

Row 14 K7, p1, k1, p2, k4, p7, k4.

Row 15 P4, k3, yo, k1, yo, k3, p4, k2, p1, M1 purl, k1, p2tog, p5—28 sts.

Row 16 K6, p1, k2, p2, k4, p9, k4.

Row 17 P4, ssk, k5, k2tog, p4, k2, p1, M1 purl, p1, k1, p2tog, p4—26 sts.

Row 18 K5, p1, k3, p2, k4, p7, k4.

Row 19 P4, ssk, k3, k2tog, p4, k2, p1, M1 purl, p2, k1, p2tog, p3—24 sts.

Row 20 K4, p1, k4, p2, k4, p5, k4.

Row 21 P4, ssk, k1, k2tog, p4, k2, p4, yo, k1, yo, p4.

Row 22 K4, p3, k4, p2, k4, p3, k4.

Row 23 P4, S2KP, p2, p2tog, k1, yo, k1, p4, yo, k1, yo, k2, p4.

Row 24 K4, p5, k4, p3, k8.

Rep rows 1–24.

Stitch Key

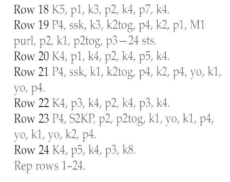

☐ K on RS, p on WS	◹ K2tog	M Make 1 purl
— P on RS, k on WS	◸ P2tog	⋏ S2KP
○ Yo	◺ Ssk	

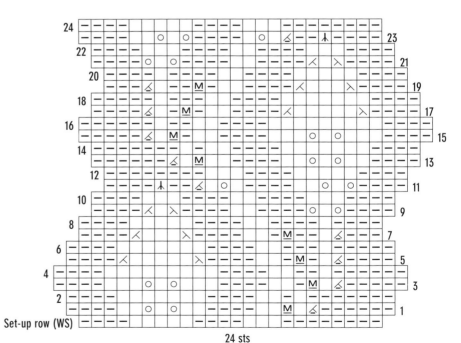

24 sts

Set-up row (WS)

126 double leaves

(worked over 31 sts)

Row 1 (RS) Yo, k2tog, yo, k1, yo, k4, S2KP, k4, yo, S2KP, yo, k4, S2KP, k4, yo, k1, yo, ssk, yo.

Row 2 and all WS rows Purl.

Row 3 Yo, k2tog, [yo, k3] twice, S2KP, k3, yo, S2KP, yo, k3, S2KP, [k3, yo] twice, ssk, yo.

Row 5 Yo, k2tog, yo, k5, yo, k2, S2KP, k2, yo, S2KP, yo, k2, S2KP, k2, yo, k5, yo, ssk, yo.

Row 7 Yo, k2tog, yo, k7, yo, k1, S2KP, k1, yo, S2KP, yo, k1, S2KP, k1, yo, k7, yo, ssk, yo.

Row 9 Yo, k2tog, yo, k9, [yo, S2KP] 3 times, yo, k9, yo, ssk, yo.

Row 11 Yo, k2tog, yo, k10, k2tog, yo, S2KP, yo, ssk, k10, yo, ssk, yo.

Row 12 Purl.

Rep rows 1–12.

Stitch Key

☐	K on RS, p on WS
⊙	Yo
╱	K2tog
╲	Ssk
人	S2KP

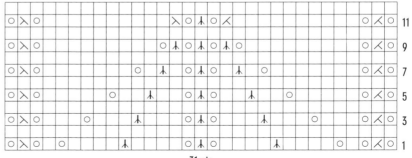

31 sts

126

127 vertebrae

Ssk and pass Ssk, return resulting st to LH needle and pass 2nd st on LH needle over first st, then sl st back to RH needle.

(worked over 25 sts)

Row 1 (RS) K6, ssk and pass, yo, k1, yo, p1, yo, ssk and pass, yo, p1, yo, k1, yo, SK2P, k6.

Rows 2, 4 and 6 P10, k1, p3, k1, p10.

Row 3 K4, ssk and pass, [k1, yo] twice, k1, p1, yo, ssk and pass, yo, p1, [k1, yo] twice, k1, SK2P, k4.

Row 5 K2, ssk and pass, k2, yo, k1, yo, k2, p1, yo, ssk and pass, yo, p1, k2, yo, k1, yo, k2, SK2P, k2.

Row 7 Ssk and pass, k3, yo, k1, yo, k3, p1, yo, ssk and pass, yo, p1, k3, yo, k1, yo, k3, SK2P.

Row 8 Rep row 2.

Rep rows 1–8.

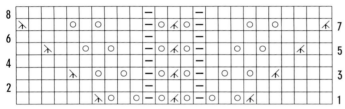

25 sts

Stitch Key

☐	K on RS, p on WS
▬	P on RS, k on WS
⊙	Yo
⋏	SK2P
⊼	Ssk and pass

127

128 candle flame

(worked over 15 sts)
Row 1 (RS) Ssp, p5, yo, k1, yo, p5, p2tog.
Row 2 K6, p3, k6.
Row 3 Ssp, p4, [k1, yo] twice, k1, p4, p2tog.
Row 4 K5, p5, k5.
Row 5 Ssp, p3, k2, yo, k1, yo, k2, p3, p2tog.
Row 6 K4, p7, k4.
Row 7 Ssp, p2, k3, yo, k1, yo, k3, p2, p2tog.
Row 8 K3, p9, k3.
Row 9 P1, yo, p2, k3, S2KP, k3, p2, yo, p1.
Row 10 K4, p7, k4.
Row 11 P1, yo, p3, k2, S2KP, k2, p3, yo, p1.
Row 12 K5, p5, k5.
Row 13 P1, yo, p4, k1, S2KP, k1, p4, yo, p1.
Row 14 K6, p3, k6.
Row 15 P1, yo, p5,S2KP, p5, yo, p1.
Row 16 K7, p1, k7.
Rep rows 1–16.

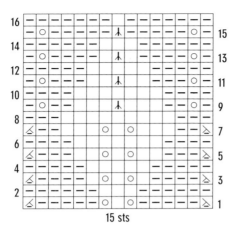

15 sts

Stitch Key

☐	K on RS, p on WS
─	P on RS, k on WS
○	Yo
◿	P2tog
◺	Ssp
⋏	S2KP

128

129 caterpillar

2-st RT K2tog, leave sts on LH needle,
k first st again, sl both sts from needle.
(worked over 10 sts)
Row 1 (RS) K2, k2tog, yo, 2-st RT, yo, ssk, k2.
Rows 2, 4 and 8 Purl.
Row 3 K1, k2tog, yo, k4, yo, ssk, k1.
Row 5 K2tog, yo, k1, k2tog, yo twice, ssk, k1, yo, ssk.
Row 6 P4, k1 into first yo, p1 into 2nd yo, p4.
Row 7 K2, yo, ssk, k2, k2tog, yo, k2.
Row 9 K3, yo, ssk, k2tog yo, k3.
Row 10 Purl.
Rep rows 1–10.

Stitch Key

☐	K on RS, p on WS	◿	K2tog
─	K on WS	◺	Ssk
○	Yo	⤢	2-st RT

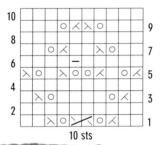

10 sts

129

131

130 open book

(worked over 48 sts)

Row 1 (RS) K1, [k3, (k2tog) twice, yo, k1, yo] twice, k4, k2tog, yo, k2, yo, ssk, k4, [yo, k1, yo, (ssk) twice, k3] twice, k1.

Rows 2, 4 and 6 Purl.

Row 3 K2, [k2tog] twice, yo, k1, yo, [k3, (k2tog) twice, yo, k1, yo] twice, k2, [yo, k1, yo, (ssk) twice, k3] twice, yo, k1, yo, [ssk] twice, k2.

Row 5 [(k2tog) twice, yo, k1, yo, k3] 3 times, [k3, yo, k1, yo, (ssk) twice] 3 times.

Row 7 K6, [(k2tog) twice, yo, k1, yo, k3] twice, k7, [yo, k1, yo, (ssk) twice, k3] twice, k3.

Row 8 Purl.

Rep rows 1–8.

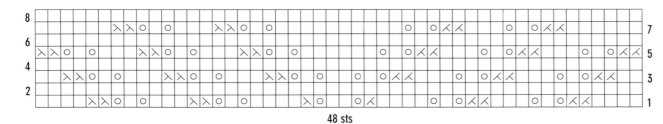

48 sts

Stitch Key

□	K on RS, p on WS
⊡	Yo
⊠	K2tog
⊠	Ssk

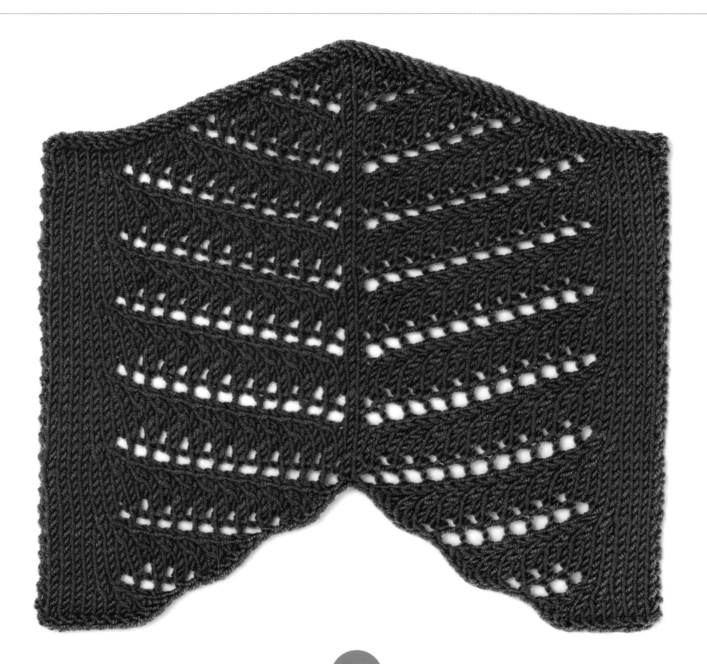

131 do the twist

(worked over 16 sts)
Row 1 (RS) K5, yo, ssk, k2, yo, ssk, k5.
Row 2 and all WS rows Purl.
Row 3 K3, k2tog, yo, k1, yo, ssk, k2, yo, ssk, k4.
Row 5 K2, k2tog, yo, k3, yo, ssk, k2, yo, ssk, k3.
Row 7 K1, k2tog, yo, k2, k2tog, yo, k1, [yo, ssk, k2] twice.

Row 9 K2tog, yo, k2, k2tog, yo, k3, yo, ssk, k2, yo, ssk, k1.
Row 11 [K2, yo, ssk] twice, yo, k2tog, yo, k2, k2tog, yo, k2tog.
Row 13 K3, yo, ssk, k2, yo, SK2P, yo, k2, k2tog, yo, k2.
Row 15 K4, yo, ssk, k2, yo, ssk, k1, k2tog, yo, k3.
Row 16 Purl.
Rep rows 1–16.

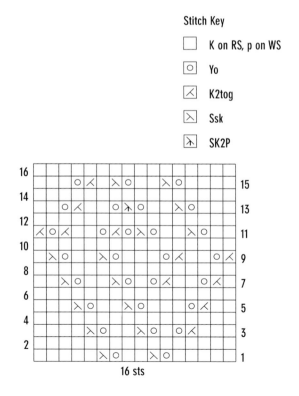

Stitch Key

☐ K on RS, p on WS

⊡ Yo

╱ K2tog

╲ Ssk

⋏ SK2P

16 sts

132 hearts entwined

(worked over 20 sts)
Row 1 (RS) K4, [yo, ssk] twice, k3, [k2tog, yo] twice, k5.
Row 2 and all WS rows Purl.
Row 3 K2, [k2tog, yo] twice, k4, [k2tog, yo] twice, k1, yo, ssk, k3.
Row 5 K1, [k2tog, yo] twice, k4, [k2tog, yo] twice, k1, [yo, ssk] twice, k2.
Row 7 [K2tog, yo] twice, k4, [k2tog, yo] twice, k3, [yo, ssk] twice, k1.
Row 9 K2, [yo, ssk] twice, k1, [k2tog, yo] twice, k5, [yo, ssk] twice.
Row 11 K3, yo, ssk, yo, SK2P, yo, k2tog, yo, k4, [k2tog, yo] twice, k2.
Row 13 K4, yo, ssk, yo, SK2P, yo, k4, [k2tog, yo] twice, k3.
Row 15 K5, [yo, ssk] twice, k3, [k2tog, yo] twice, k4.

Row 17 K3, k2tog, yo, k1, [yo, ssk] twice, k4, [yo, ssk] twice, k2.
Row 19 K2, [k2tog, yo] twice, k1, [yo, ssk] twice, k4, [yo, ssk] twice, k1.
Row 21 K1, [k2tog, yo] twice, k3, [yo, ssk] twice, k4, [yo, ssk] twice.
Row 23 [K2tog, yo] twice, k5, [yo, ssk] twice, k1, [k2tog, yo] twice, k2.
Row 25 K2, [yo, ssk] twice, k4, yo, ssk, yo, k3tog, yo, k2tog, yo, k3.
Row 27 K3, [yo, ssk] twice, k4, yo, k3tog, yo, k2tog, yo, k4.
Row 28 Purl.
Rep rows 1–28.

Stitch Key

☐ K on RS, p on WS

◉ Yo

╱ K2tog

⫽ K3tog

╲ Ssk

⋏ SK2P

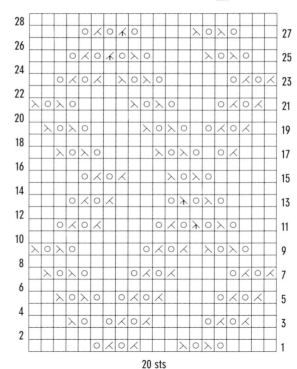

20 sts

133 reversible frost flowers

(worked over 34 sts)

Note Sl sts purlwise with yarn at WS of work.

Row 1 (RS) Sl 2, p3, ssp, k4, yo, k2, yo, ssk, p2, yo, p2tog, k2, yo, ssk, yo, k4, p2tog, p3, k2.

Row 2 Sl 2, k2, k2tog, p4, yo, k1, p2, yo, p2tog, k2, yo, ssk, p2, yo, p2tog, k1, yo, p4, ssk, k2, p2.

Row 3 Sl 2, p1, ssp, k4, yo, p2, k2, yo, ssk, p2, yo, p2tog, k2, yo, ssk, p2, yo, k4, p2tog, pl, k2.

Row 4 Sl 2, k2tog, p4, yo, k3, p2, yo, p2tog, k2, yo, ssk, p2, yo, p2tog, k3, yo, p4, ssk, p2.

Row 5 Sl 2, k3, k2tog, p4, yo, k2, yo, ssk, p2, yo, p2tog, k2, yo, ssk, yo, p4, ssk, k5.

Row 6 Sl 2, p2, ssp, k4, yo, p3, yo, p2tog, k2, yo, ssk, p2, yo, p2tog, pl, yo, k4, p2tog, p4.

Row 7 Sl 2, k1, k2tog, p4, yo, k4, yo, ssk, p2, yo, p2tog, k2, yo, ssk, k2, yo, p4, ssk, k3.

Row 8 Sl 2, ssp, k4, yo, p5, yo, p2tog, k2, yo, ssk, p2, yo, p2tog, p3, yo, k4, p2tog, p2.

Rows 9–16 Rep rows 1–8.

Row 17 Sl 2, yo, ssk, p2, yo, p2tog, yo, k4, p2tog, p6, ssp, k4, yo, p2, yo, p2tog, yo, ssk, k2.

Row 18 Sl 2, p2, k2, yo, ssk, k1, yo, p4, ssk, k4, k2tog, p4, yo, k3, yo, ssk, p4.

Row 19 Sl 2, yo, ssk, p2, yo, p2tog, p2, yo, k4, p2tog, p2, ssp, k4, yo, p4, yo, p2tog, yo, ssk, k2.

Row 20 Sl 2, p2, k2, yo, ssk, k3, yo, p4, ssk, k2tog, p4, yo, k5, yo, ssk, p4.

Row 21 Sl 2, yo, ssk, p2, yo, p2tog, yo, p4, ssk, k6, k2tog, p4, yo, p2, yo, p2tog, yo, ssk, k2.

Row 22 Sl 2, p2, k2, yo, ssk, pl, yo, k4, p2tog, p4, ssp, k4, yo, pl, k2, yo, ssk, p4.

Row 23 Sl 2, yo, ssk, p2, yo, p2tog, k2, yo, p4, ssk, k2, k2tog, p4, yo, k2, p2, yo, p2tog, yo, ssk, k2.

Row 24 Sl 2, p2, k2, yo, ssk, p3, yo, k4, p2tog, ssp, k4, yo, p3, k2, yo, ssk, p4.

Rows 25–32 Rep rows 17–24.

Rep rows 1–32.

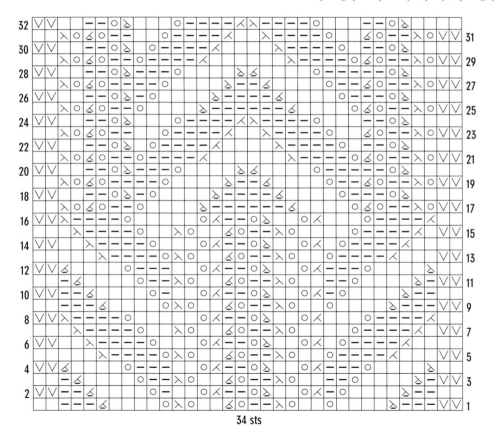

Stitch Key

☐	K on RS, p on WS
—	P on RS, k on WS
○	Yo
╱	K2tog on RS, p2tog on WS
◢	P2tog on RS, k2tog on WS
╲	Ssk on RS, ssp on WS
◣	Ssp on RS, ssk on WS
∨	Sl 1 purlwise with yarn at WS of work

134 o christmas tree

Make Bobble (MB) K into front, back and front of st, turn, p3, turn, SK2P.
(worked over 23 sts)
Row 1 (RS) P1, k8, k2tog, yo, k1, yo, SKP, k8, p1.
Row 2 and all WS rows K1, p21, k1.
Row 3 P1, k4, MB, k2, k2tog, yo, k3, yo, SKP, k2, MB, k4, p1.
Row 5 P1, k6, [k2tog, yo] twice, k1, [yo, SKP] twice, k6, p1.
Row 7 P1, k2, MB, k2, [k2tog, yo] twice, k3, [yo, SKP] twice, k2, MB, k2, p1.
Row 9 P1, k4, [k2tog, yo] 3 times, k1, [yo, SKP] 3 times, k4, p1.
Row 11 P1, MB, k4, [k2tog, yo] twice, k3, [yo, SKP] twice, k4, MB, p1.
Row 13 Rep row 5.
Rows 15–19 Rep rows 3–7.
Row 21 Rep row 5.
Row 23 Rep row 3.
Row 25 Rep row 1.
Row 27 P1, k2, MB, k2, yo, SKP, k3, yo, SKP, k2, k2tog, yo, k2, MB, k2, p1.
Row 29 P1, k3, k2tog, yo, k1, yo, SKP, k5, k2tog, yo, k1, yo, SKP, k3, p1.
Row 31 P1, k2, k2tog, yo, k3, yo, SKP, k3, k2tog, yo, k3, yo, SKP, k2, p1.
Row 33 P1, k3, SKP, yo, k1, yo, k2tog, k2, MB, k2, SKP, yo, k1, yo, k2tog, k3, p1.
Row 35 P1, k5, yo, k2tog, k7, SKP, yo, k5, p1.
Row 36 Rep row 2.
Rep rows 1–36.

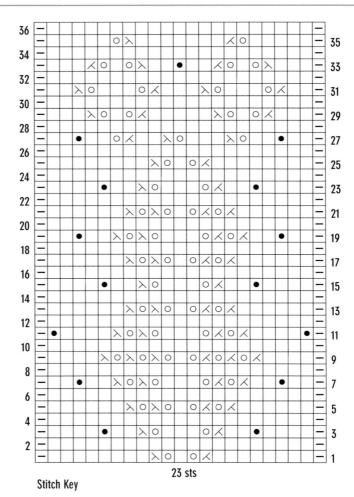

23 sts

Stitch Key

☐ K on RS, p on WS

─ P on RS, k on WS

○ Yo

╱ K2tog

╲ SKP

● MB

134

135 trefoil

3-into-9 Flower [K3tog but do not remove sts from LH needle, yo] 4 times (working into the same 3 sts each time), k same 3 sts tog once more and drop from LH needle—9 sts.

(worked over 23 sts)

Row 1 (RS) Yo, k3tog, yo, k1, k3tog, [k3, yo] twice, k3, sssk, k1, yo, sssk, yo—21 sts.

Row 2 and all WS rows Purl.

Row 3 Yo, k3tog, yo, k2tog, yo, k2, k2tog, yo, k3, yo, ssk, k2, yo, ssk, yo, sssk, yo.

Row 5 Yo, k3tog, yo, k2tog, yo, k3tog, yo, k1, yo, k3, yo, k1, yo, sssk, yo, ssk, yo, sssk, yo.

Row 7 Yo, k3tog, yo, k1, [k2tog, yo] twice, k1, yo, S2KP, yo, k1, [yo, ssk] twice, k1, yo, sssk, yo.

Row 9 Yo, k3tog, yo, [k2tog, yo] twice, k2, yo, k3tog, yo, k2, [yo, ssk] twice, yo, sssk, yo.

Row 11 Yo, k3tog, yo, k2tog, yo, k1, k3tog, 3-into-9 Flower, sssk, k1, yo, ssk, yo, sssk, yo—23 sts.

Row 12 Purl.

Rep rows 1–12.

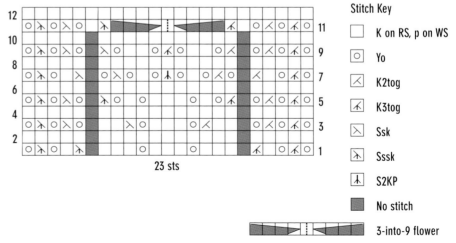

Stitch Key

☐	K on RS, p on WS
⊙	Yo
╱	K2tog
⪢	K3tog
╲	Ssk
⪡	Sssk
⋏	S2KP
▨	No stitch
	3-into-9 flower

23 sts

combos

7-st LC Sl 4 sts to cn and hold to *front*, k3, k4 from cn.

(multiple of 20 sts plus 13)

Row 1 (RS) K6, *yo, ssk, k18; rep from *, end last rep k5 (instead of 18).

Row 2 and all WS rows Purl.

Row 3 *K4, k2tog, yo, k1, yo, ssk, k4, 7-st LC; rep from * to last 13 sts, end k4, k2tog, yo, k1, yo, ssk, k4.

Row 5 K3, *k2tog, yo, k1, [yo, ssk] twice, k13; rep from *, end last rep k3 (instead of 13).

Row 7 *K2, k2tog, yo, k5, yo, ssk, k2, 7-st LC; rep from * to last 13 sts, end k2, k2tog, yo, k5, yo, ssk, k2.

Row 9 K2, *yo, ssk, k5, k2tog, yo, k11; rep from *, end last rep k2 (instead of 11).

Row 11 *K3, yo, ssk, k3, k2tog, yo, k3, 7-st LC; rep from * to last 13 sts, end k3, yo, ssk, k3, k2tog, yo, k3.

Row 13 K4, *yo, ssk, k1, k2tog, yo, k15; rep from *, end last rep k4 (instead of 15).

Row 15 *K5, yo, SK2P, yo, k5, 7-st LC; rep from * to last 13 sts, end k5, yo, SK2P, yo, k5.

Row 16 Purl.

Rep rows 1–16.

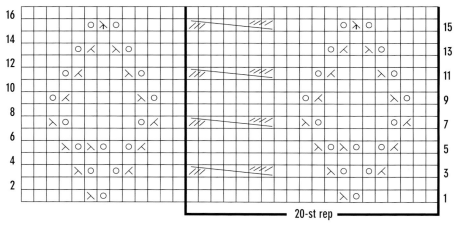

20-st rep

Stitch Key

	K on RS, p on WS
⊡	Yo
⊠	K2tog
⊠	Ssk
⊠	SK2P
	7-st LC

136

combos

6-st RC Sl 6 sts to RH needle, dropping extra wraps, sl same 6 sts back to LH needle, then sl 3 sts to cn and hold to *back*, k3, k3 from cn.

(multiple of 6 sts)

Row 1 (WS) Knit.

Row 2 *K1, wrapping yarn 3 times around needle (instead of once); rep from *.

Row 3 *6-st RC; rep from *.

Row 4 Knit.

Rep rows 1–4.

5-st LC Sl 2 sts to cn and hold to *front*, k3, k2 from cn.

(multiple of 16 sts plus 1)

Row 1 (RS) P1, *k2tog, yo, k5, yo, ssk, p1, k5, p1; rep from * to end.

Rows 2, 4 and 6 *K1, p5, k1, p9; rep from *, end k1.

Row 3 P1, *k2, yo, ssk, k1, k2tog, yo, k2, p1, k5, p1; rep from * to end.

Row 5 P1, *k3, yo, S2KP, yo, k3, p1, 5-st LC, p1; rep from * to end.

Row 7 P1, *k1, k2tog, yo, k3, yo, ssk, k1, p1, k5, p1; rep from * to end.

Row 8 Rep row 2.

Rep rows 1–8.

Stitch Key

☐	K on RS
⊟	K on WS
⧄	K1, wrapping yarn 3 times around needle

☒ 6-st RC

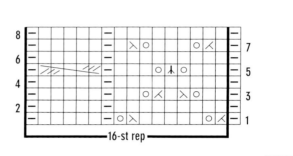

Stitch Key

☐	K on RS, p on WS
⊟	P on RS, k on WS
⊙	Yo
⟋	K2tog
⟍	Ssk
⋏	S2KP

☒ 5-st LC

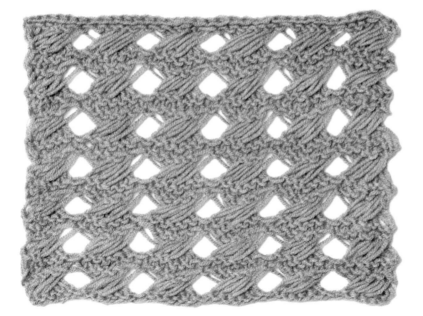

139 lover's knot

6-st RC Sl 3 sts to cn and hold to *back*, k3, k3 from cn.
(worked over 20 sts)
Row 1 (RS) K4, yo, k2, ssk, k4, k2tog, k2, yo, k4.
Row 2 and all WS rows Purl.
Row 3 K5, yo, k2, ssk, k2, k2tog, k2, yo, k5.
Row 5 K1, yo, k2, ssk, k1, yo, k2, ssk, k2tog, k2, yo, k1, k2tog, k2, yo, k1.
Row 7 K2, yo, k2, ssk, k1, 6-st RC, k1, k2tog, k2, yo, k2.
Row 9 K3, yo, k2, ssk, k6, k2tog, k2, yo, k3.

Row 11 K3, k2tog, k2, yo, k6, yo, k2, ssk, k3.
Row 13 K2, k2tog, k2, yo, k8, yo, k2, ssk, k2.
Row 15 K1, k2tog, k2, yo, k2, 6-st RC, k2, yo, k2, ssk, k1.
Row 17 Knit.
Row 19 K5, k2tog, k2, yo, k2, yo, k2, ssk, k5.
Row 21 K4, k2tog, k2, yo, k4, yo, k2, ssk, k4.
Row 22 Purl.
Rep rows 1–22.

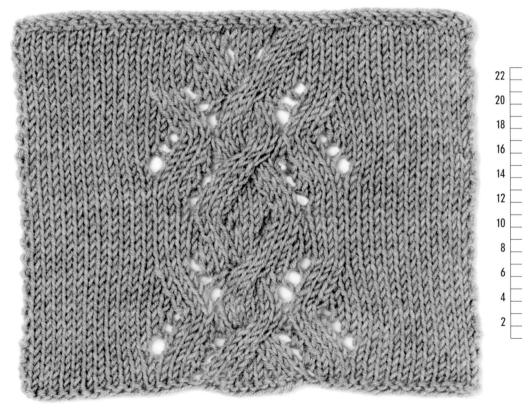

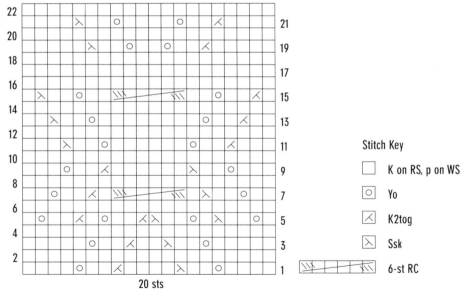

20 sts

Stitch Key

☐	K on RS, p on WS
⊡	Yo
⟋	K2tog
⟍	Ssk
⟍⟍⟍╱	6-st RC

combos

2-st RT Sl 1 st to cn and hold to *back*, k1, k1 from cn.
(multiple of 15 sts plus 1)
Row 1 (RS) K1, *yo, k3, k2tog, k1, 2-st RT, k1, ssk, k3,
yo, p1; rep from *, end last rep k1 (instead of p1).
Rows 2, 4 and 6 K1, *p5, k1, p2, k1, p5, k1;
rep from * to end.
Row 3 K1, *k1, yo, k2, k2tog, k1, 2-st RT, k1, ssk, k2,
yo, k1, p1; rep from *, end last rep k2 (instead of k1, p1).

Row 5 K1, *k2, yo, k1, k2tog, k1, 2-st RT, k1, ssk, k1, yo,
k2, p1; rep from *, end last rep k3 (instead of k2, p1).
Row 7 K1, *k3, yo, k2tog, k1, 2-st RT, k1, ssk, yo, k3, p1;
rep from *, end last rep k4 (instead of k3, p1).
Row 8 Rep row 2.
Rep rows 1–8.

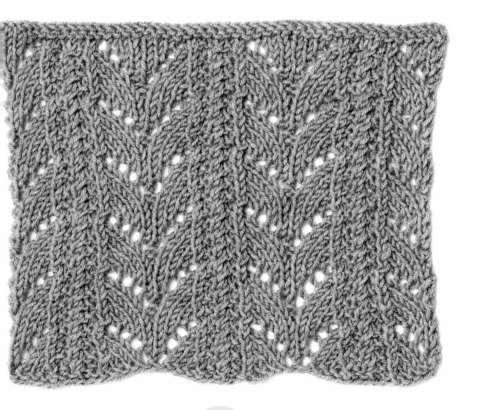

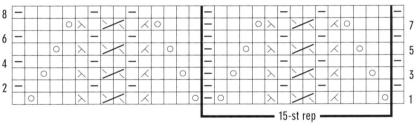

15-st rep

Stitch Key

☐ K on RS, p on WS

— P on RS, k on WS

○ Yo

⟋ K2tog

⟍ Ssk

⟋ 2-st RT

2-st RT Sl 1 st to cn and hold to *back*, k1, k1 from cn.
2-st LT Sl 1 st to cn and hold to *front*, k1, k1 from cn.
(multiple of 22 sts)
Row 1 (RS) *K4, 2-st RT, p1, k2tog, yo, k1, p1, 2-st LT, k4, p1, k2tog, yo, k1, p1; rep from * to end.
Row 2 and all WS rows *K1, p3, k1, p6; rep from * to end.
Row 3 *K3, 2-st RT, k1, p1, k1, yo, ssk, p1, k1, 2-st LT, k3, p1, k1, yo, ssk, p1; rep from * to end.
Row 5 *K2, [2-st RT] twice, p1, k2tog, yo, k1, p1, [2-st LT] twice, k2, p1, k2tog, yo, k1, p1; rep from * to end.
Row 7 *K1, [2-st RT] twice, k1, p1, k1, yo, ssk, p1, k1, [2-st LT] twice, k1, p1, k1, yo, ssk, p1; rep from * to end.

Row 9 *[2-st RT] twice, k2, p1, k2tog, yo, k1, p1, k2, [2-st LT] twice, p1, k2tog, yo, k1, p1; rep from * to end.
Row 11 *K1, 2-st RT, k3, p1, k1, yo, ssk, p1, k3, 2-st LT, k1, p1, k1, yo, ssk, p1; rep from * to end.
Row 13 *2-st RT, k4, p1, k2tog, yo, k1, p1, k4, 2-st LT, p1, k2tog, yo, k1, p1; rep from * to end.
Row 15 *K4, 2-st RT, p1, k1, yo, ssk, p1, 2-st LT, k4, p1, k1, yo, ssk, p1; rep from * to end.
Row 17 *K3, 2-st RT, k1, p1, k2tog, yo, k1, p1, k1, 2-st LT, k3, p1, k2tog, yo, k1, p1; rep from * to end.
Row 19 *K2, [2-st RT] twice, p1, k1, yo, ssk, p1, [2-st LT] twice, k2, p1, k1, yo, ssk, p1; rep from * to end.

Row 21 *K1, [2-st RT] twice, k1, p1, k2tog, yo, k1, p1, k1, [2-st LT] twice, k1, p1, k2tog, yo, k1, p1; rep from * to end.
Row 23 *[2-st RT] twice, k2, p1, k1, yo, ssk, p1, k2, [2-st LT] twice, p1, k1, yo, ssk, p1; rep from * to end.
Row 25 *K1, 2-st RT, k3, p1, k2tog, yo, k1, p1, k3, 2-st LT, k1, p1, k2tog, yo, k1, p1; rep from * to end.
Row 27 *2-st RT, k4, p1, k1, yo, ssk, p1, k4, 2-st LT, p1, k1, yo, ssk, p1; rep from * to end.
Row 28 Rep row 2.
Rep rows 1–28.

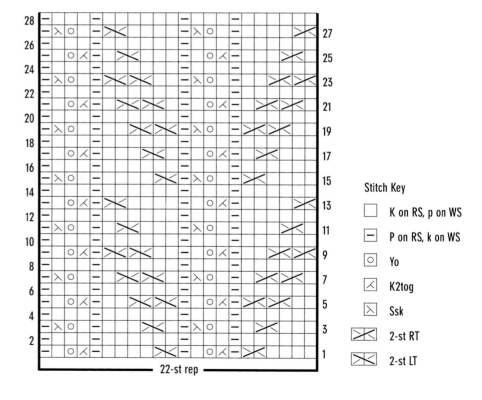

Stitch Key

☐ K on RS, p on WS

— P on RS, k on WS

○ Yo

⟋ K2tog

⟍ Ssk

⧗ 2-st RT

⧓ 2-st LT

22-st rep

141

combos

6-st RC Sl 3 sts to cn and hold to *back*, k3, k3 from cn.
(multiple of 11 sts plus 7)

Rows 1 and 5 (RS) K1, *yo, SKP, k1, k2tog, yo, k6; rep from *, end last rep k1 (instead of 6).

Row 2 and all WS rows K1, p to last st, k1.

Row 3 K2, yo, S2KP, yo, k1, *6-st RC, k1, yo, S2KP, yo, k1; rep from *, end k1.

Row 7 K1, *k1, yo, S2KP, yo, k7; rep from *, end last rep k2 (instead of 7).

Row 9 K1, yo, SKP, k1, k2tog, yo, *6-st RC, yo, SKP, k1, k2tog, yo; rep from *, end k1.

Row 11 Rep row 7.

Row 12 Rep row 2.

Rep rows 1–12.

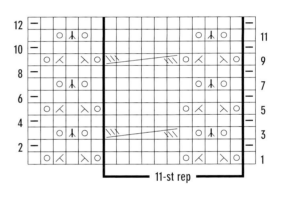

Stitch Key

☐	K on RS, p on WS
—	K on WS
○	Yo
╱	K2tog
╲	SKP
⋏	S2KP
	6-st RC

143 double helix

4-st LC Sl 2 sts to cn and hold to *front*, k2, k2 from cn.
4-st RPC Sl 2 sts to cn and hold to *back*, k2, p2 from cn.
4-st LPC Sl 2 sts to cn and hold to *front*, p2, k2 from cn.
(worked over 12 sts)
(Note On WS rows, drop the extra yo when working a st above a double yo.)
Row 1 (RS) Yo twice, p2tog, p2, 4-st LC, p2, ssp, yo twice.
Row 2 P1, k3, p4, k3, p1.
Row 3 Yo twice, p2tog, 4-st RPC, 4-st LPC, ssp, yo twice.
Rows 4, 6, 8, 10, 12, 14 and 16 P1, k1, p2, k4, p2, k1, p1.
Rows 5, 7, 9, 11, 13 and 15 Yo twice, p2tog, k2, yo, p2tog, ssp, yo, k2, ssp, yo twice.
Row 17 Yo twice, p2tog, 4-st LPC, 4-st RPC, ssp, yo twice.
Row 18 Rep row 2.
Rep rows 1–18.

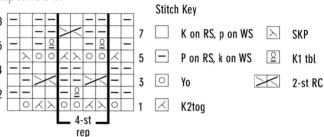

12 sts

Stitch Key

☐	K on RS, p on WS
—	P on RS, k on WS
⊙	Yo
⊙⊙	Yo twice (on WS rows, drop the extra yo)
⬈	P2tog
⬔	Ssp
⤬	4-st LC
⤬	4-st RPC
⤬	4-st LPC

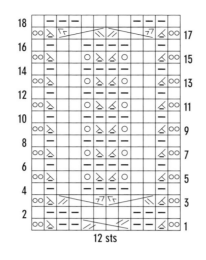

144 crisscross

2-st RC Sl 1 st to cn and hold to *back*, k1, k1 from cn.
(multiple of 4 sts plus 2)
Row 1 (RS) K1, *yo, SKP, k2tog, yo; rep from *, end k1.
Row 2 K2, p2, *k1, k1 tbl, p2; rep from *, end k2.
Row 3 K1, p1, *2-st RC, p2; rep from *, end 2-st RC, p1, k1.
Row 4 *K2, p2; rep from *, end k2.
Row 5 K1, *k2tog, yo twice, SKP; rep from *, end k1.
Row 6 K1, p1, k1, k1 tbl, *p2, k1, k1 tbl; rep from *, end p1, k1.
Row 7 K2, *p2, 2-st RC; rep from *, end p2, k2.
Row 8 K1, p1, k2, *p2, k2; rep from *, end p1, k1.
Rep rows 1–8.

4-st rep

Stitch Key

☐	K on RS, p on WS	⬊	SKP
—	P on RS, k on WS	⚎	K1 tbl
⊙	Yo	⤬	2-st RC
⬋	K2tog		

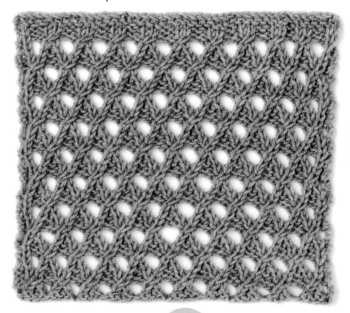

143

144

combos

12-st RC Sl 6 sts to cn and hold to *back*, k6, k6 from cn.
12-st LC Sl 6 sts to cn and hold to *front*, k6, k6 from cn.
(multiple of 20 sts plus 4)
Row 1 and all odd rows (except 7 and 19) (RS) K4, p2, k2, *p1, yo, ssk, k2, k2tog, yo, p1, k2; rep from * to last 6 sts, end p2, k4.
Row 2 and all even rows *P4, k2, p2, k2; rep from *, end p4.

Row 7 K4, p2, k2, *p1, yo, ssk, k2, k2tog, yo, p1, 12-st LC; rep from * to last 16 sts, end p1, yo, ssk, k2, k2tog, yo, p1, k2, p2, k4.
Row 19 K4, p2, *12-st RC, p1, yo, ssk, k2, k2tog, yo, p1; rep from * to last 18 sts, end 12-st RC, p2, k4.
Row 24 Rep row 2.
Rep rows 1–24.

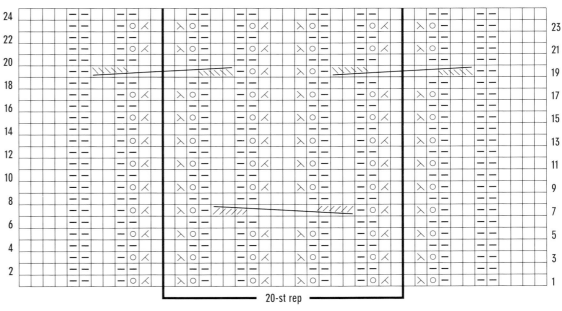

20-st rep

Stitch Key

☐	K on RS, p on WS
—	P on RS, k on WS
⊙	Yo
⊘	K2tog
⊠	Ssk

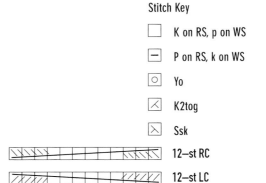

12–st RC

12–st LC

Right Lifted Inc (RLI) K into right loop of st in row below next st on LH needle, then k st on needle.

Left Lifted Inc (LLI) K next st on LH needle, then k into left loop of st in row below st just knit.

(multiple of 15 sts plus 9)

Row 1 (RS) K2, *yo, k2tog, p1, ssk, yo, LLI, k2, ssk, k5; rep from * to last 7 sts, end yo, k2tog, p1, ssk, yo, k2.

Row 2 and all WS rows Purl.

Row 3 K2, *yo, k2tog, p1, ssk, yo, k1, LLI, k2, ssk, k4; rep from * to last 7 sts, end yo, k2tog, p1, ssk, yo, k2.

Row 5 K2, *yo, k2tog, p1, ssk, yo, k2, LLI, k2, ssk, k3; rep from * to last 7 sts, end yo, k2tog, p1, ssk, yo, k2.

Row 7 K2, *yo, k2tog, p1, ssk, yo, k3, LLI, k2, ssk, k2; rep from * to last 7 sts, end yo, k2tog, p1, ssk, yo, k2.

Row 9 K2, *yo, k2tog, p1, ssk, yo, k4, LLI, k2, ssk, k1; rep from * to last 7 sts, end yo, k2tog, p1, ssk, yo, k2.

Row 11 K2, *yo, k2tog, p1, ssk, yo, k5, LLI, k2, ssk; rep from * to last 7 sts, end yo, k2tog, p1, ssk, yo, k2.

Row 13 K2, *yo, k2tog, p1, ssk, yo, k5, k2tog, k2, RLI; rep from * to last 7 sts, end yo, k2tog, p1, ssk, yo, k2.

Row 15 K2, *yo, k2tog, p1, ssk, yo, k4, k2tog, k2, RLI, k1; rep from * to last 7 sts, end yo, k2tog, p1, ssk, yo, k2.

Row 17 K2, *yo, k2tog, p1, ssk, yo, k3, k2tog, k2, RLI, k2; rep from * to last 7 sts, end yo, k2tog, p1, ssk, yo, k2.

Row 19 K2, *yo, k2tog, p1, ssk, yo, k2, k2tog, k2, RLI, k3; rep from * to last 7 sts, end yo, k2tog, p1, ssk, yo, k2.

Row 21 K2, *yo, k2tog, p1, ssk, yo, k1, k2tog, k2, RLI, k4; rep from * to last 7 sts, end yo, k2tog, p1, ssk, yo, k2.

Row 23 K2, *yo, k2tog, p1, ssk, yo, k2tog, k2, RLI, k5; rep from * to last 7 sts, end yo, k2tog, p1, ssk, yo, k2.

Row 24 Purl.

Rep rows 1–24.

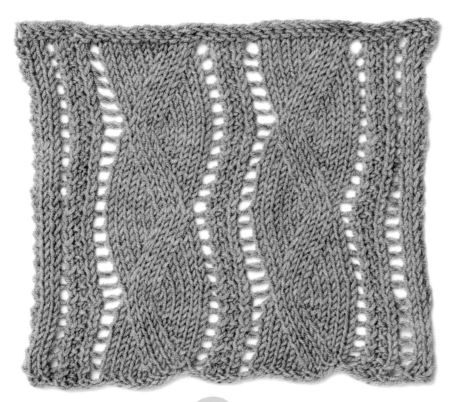

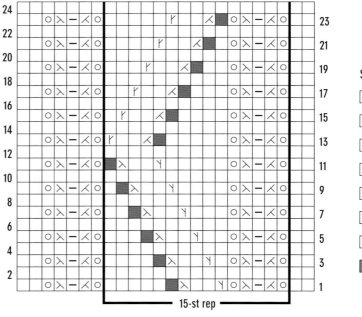

Stitch Key

☐ K on RS, p on WS

— P on RS

◯ Yo

K2tog

Ssk

Left Lifted Inc (LLI)

Right Lifted Inc (RLI)

■ No stitch

15-st rep

combos

4-st RC Sl 2 sts to cn and hold to *back*, k2, k2 from cn.
4-st LC Sl 2 sts to cn and hold to *front*, k2, k2 from cn.
8-st LC Sl 6 sts to cn and hold to *front*, k2, k6 from cn.
Notes 1) Pattern has 3 separate sections which are worked simultaneously and in this order: Right-Side Pat, Center Cable Pat, and Left-Side Pat. 2) Place markers between patterns.
Right-Side Pat (over an odd number of sts, and a minimum of 9)
Row 1 (RS) K1, *SKP, yo; rep from * to last 6 sts of pat, 4-st LC, yo, k2tog.

Rows 2 and 4 P to last st, k1.
Row 3 K1, *yo, k2tog; rep from * to last 6 sts of pat, k4, SKP, yo.
Rep rows 1–4.
Center Cable Pat (over 14 sts)
Rows 1 and 3 (RS) K14.
Row 2 and all WS rows P14.
Row 5 K1, 8-st LC, k4.
Row 7 K3, 8-st LC, k3.

Row 9 K5, 8-st LC, k1.
Row 10 P14.
Rep rows 1–10.
Left-Side Pat (over an odd number of sts, and a minimum of 9)
Row 1 (RS) SKP, yo, 4-st RC, *yo, k2tog; rep from *, end k1.
Rows 2 and 4 K1, p to end of pat.
Row 3 Yo, k2tog, k4, *SKP, yo; rep from *, end k1.
Rep rows 1–4.

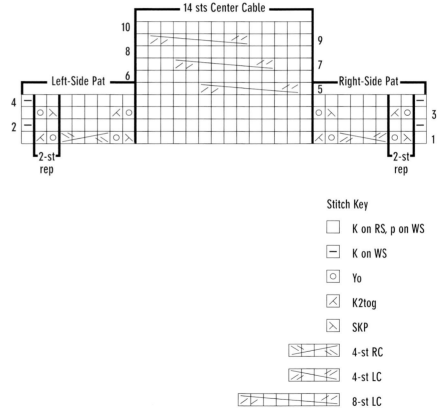

Stitch Key

☐ K on RS, p on WS

— K on WS

⊡ Yo

◺ K2tog

◹ SKP

4-st RC

4-st LC

8-st LC

2-st TRPC Sl 1 st to cn and hold to *back*, k1 tbl, p1 from cn.
2-st TLPC Sl 1 st to cn and hold to *front*, p1, k1 tbl from cn.
3-st TRPC Sl 1 st to cn and hold to *back*, k2 tbl, p1 from cn.
3-st TLPC Sl 2 sts to cn and hold to *front*, p1, k2 tbl from cn.
3-st TRKC Sl 1 st to cn and hold to *back*, k2 tbl, k1 tbl from cn.
3-st TLKC Sl 2 sts to cn and hold to *front,* k1 tbl, k2 tbl from cn.
(multiple of 24 sts plus 5)
Row 1 (RS) *K2 tbl, p2, k1 tbl, p2, yo, ssk, k5, k2tog, [p1, k1 tbl] 3 times, yo, p2; rep from * to last 5 sts, end k2 tbl, p2, k1 tbl.
Row 2 *P1 tbl, k2, p2 tbl, k2, p1, [p1 tbl, k1] 3 times, p1, k5, p2, k2; rep from * to last 5 sts, end p1 tbl, k2, p2 tbl.
Row 3 *3-st TLPC, 2-st TRPC, p2, k1, yo, ssk, k3, k2tog, [p1, k1 tbl] 3 times, yo, k1 tbl, p2; rep from * to last 5 sts, end 3-st TLPC, 2-st TRPC.
Row 4 *K1, p3 tbl, k3, [p1 tbl, k1] 4 times, p1, k3, p3, k2; rep from * to last 5 sts, end k1, p3 tbl, k1.
Row 5 *P1, 3-st TLKC, p3, [yo, ssk] twice, k1, k2tog, [p1, k1 tbl] 3 times, yo, p1, k1 tbl, p2; rep from * to last 5 sts, end p1, 3-st TLKC, p1.
Row 6 *K1, p3 tbl, k3, p1 tbl, k1, p1, [p1 tbl, k1] 3 times, p1, k1, p4, k2; rep from * to last 5 sts, end k1, p3 tbl, k1.
Row 7 *2-st TRPC, 3-st TLPC, p2, k1, yo, ssk, yo, k3tog, [p1, k1 tbl] 3 times, yo, k1 tbl, p1, k1 tbl, p2; rep from * to last 5 sts, end 2-st TRPC, 3-st TLPC.
Row 8 *P2 tbl, k2, p1 tbl, k2, [p1 tbl, k1] 5 times, p5, k2; rep from * to last 5 sts, end p2 tbl, k2, p1 tbl.
Row 9 *K1 tbl, p2, k2 tbl, p2, yo, ssk, yo, k3tog, [p1, k1 tbl] 3 times, yo, [p1, k1 tbl] twice, p2; rep from * to last 5 sts, end k1 tbl, p2, k2 tbl.
Row 10 *P2 tbl, k2, p1 tbl, k2, [p1 tbl, k1] twice, p1, [p1 tbl, k1] 3 times, p4, k2; rep from * to last 5 sts, end p2 tbl, k2, p1 tbl.
Row 11 *2-st TLPC, 3-st TRPC, p2, k1, yo, k3tog, [p1, k1 tbl] 3 times, yo, [k1 tbl, p1] twice, k1 tbl, p2; rep from * to last 5 sts, end 2-st TLPC, 3-st TRPC.

Row 12 *K1, p3 tbl, k3, [p1 tbl, k1] 6 times, p3, k2; rep from * to last 5 sts, end k1, p3 tbl, k1.
Row 13 *P1, 3-st TRKC, p3, yo, k3tog, [p1, k1 tbl] 3 times, yo, [p1, k1 tbl] 3 times, p2; rep from * to last 5 sts, end p1, 3-st TRKC, p1.
Row 14 *K1, p3 tbl, k3, [p1 tbl, k1] 3 times, p1, [p1 tbl, k1] 3 times, p2, k2; rep from * to last 5 sts, end k1, p3 tbl, k1.
Row 15 *3-st TRPC, 2-st TLPC, p2, k2tog, [p1, k1 tbl] 3 times, yo, [k1 tbl, p1] 3 times, k1 tbl, p2; rep from * to last 5 sts, end 3-st TRPC, 2-st TLPC.
Row 16 *P1 tbl, k2, p2 tbl, k2, [p1 tbl, k1] 7 times, p1, k2; rep from * to last 5 sts, end p1 tbl, k2, p2 tbl.
Row 17 *K2 tbl, p2, k1 tbl, p2, yo, [k1 tbl, p1] 3 times, ssk, k5, k2tog, yo, p2; rep from * to last 5 sts, end k2 tbl, p2, k1 tbl.
Row 18 *P1 tbl, k2, p2 tbl, k2, p2, k5, p1, [k1, p1 tbl] 3 times, p1, k2; rep from * to last 5 sts, end p1 tbl, k2, p2 tbl.
Row 19 *3-st TLPC, 2-st TRPC, p2, k1 tbl, yo, [k1 tbl, p1] 3 times, ssk, k3, k2tog, yo, k1, p2; rep from * to last 5 sts, end 3-st TLPC, 2-st TRPC.
Row 20 *K1, p3 tbl, k3, p3, k3, p1, [k1, p1 tbl] 4 times, k2; rep from * to last 5 sts, end k1, p3 tbl, k1.
Row 21 *P1, 3-st TLKC, p3, k1 tbl, p1, yo, [k1 tbl, p1] 3 times, ssk, k1, [k2tog, yo] twice, p2; rep from * to last 5 sts, end p1, 3-st TLKC, p1.
Row 22 *K1, p3 tbl, k3, p4 k1, p1, [k1, p1 tbl] 3 times, p1, k1, p1 tbl, k2; rep from * to last 5 sts, end k1, p3 tbl, k1.
Row 23 *2-st TRPC, 3-st TLPC, p2, k1 tbl, p1, k1 tbl, yo, [k1 tbl, p1] 3 times, SK2P, yo, k2tog, yo, k1, p2; rep from * to last 5 sts, end 2-st TRPC, 3-st TLPC.
Row 24 *P2 tbl, k2, p1 tbl, k2, p5, [k1, p1 tbl] 5 times, k2; rep from * to last 5 sts, end p2 tbl, k2, p1 tbl.
Row 25 *K1 tbl, p2, k2 tbl, p2, [k1 tbl, p1] twice, yo, [k1 tbl, p1] 3 times, SK2P, yo, k2tog, yo, p2; rep from * to last 5 sts, end k1 tbl, p2, k2 tbl.

Row 26 *P2 tbl, k2, p1 tbl, k2, p4, [k1, p1 tbl] 3 times, p1, [k1, p1 tbl] twice, k2; rep from * to last 5 sts, end p2 tbl, k2, p1 tbl.
Row 27 *2-st TLPC, 3-st TRPC, p2, [k1 tbl, p1] twice, k1 tbl, yo, [k1 tbl, p1] 3 times, SK2P, yo, k1, p2; rep from * to last 5 sts, end 2-st TLPC, 3-st TRPC.
Row 28 *K1, p3 tbl, k3, p3, [k1, p1 tbl] 6 times, k2; rep from * to last 5 sts, end k1, p3 tbl, k1.
Row 29 *P1, 3-st TRKC, p3, [k1, p1 tbl] 3 times, yo, [k1, p1 tbl] 3 times, SK2P, yo, p2; rep from * to last 5 sts, end p1, 3-st TRKC, p1.
Row 30 *K1, p3 tbl, k3, p2, [k1, p1 tbl] 3 times, p1, [k1, p1 tbl] 3 times, k2; rep from * to last 5 sts, end k1, p3 tbl, k1.
Row 31 *3-st TRPC, 2-st TLPC, p2, [k1 tbl, p1] 3 times, k1 tbl, yo, [k1 tbl, p1] 3 times, ssk, p2; rep from * to last 5 sts, end 3-st TRPC, 2-st TLPC.
Row 32 *P1 tbl, k2, p2 tbl, k2, p1, [k1, p1 tbl] 3 times, p1, [p1 tbl, k1] 3 times, p1 tbl, k2; rep from * to last 5 sts, end p1 tbl, k2, p2 tbl.
Rep rows 1–32.

Chart row numbers (left side, bottom to top): 2, 4, 6, 8, 10, 12, 14, 16, 18, 20, 22, 24, 26, 28, 30, 32

Chart row numbers (right side, bottom to top): 1, 3, 5, 7, 9, 11, 13, 15, 17, 19, 21, 23, 25, 27, 29, 31

— 24-st rep —

Stitch Key

☐ K on RS, p on WS	⋏ SK2P	⊐ 3-st TRPC
— P on RS, k on WS	⋏ K3tog	⊐ 3-st TLPC
○ Yo	Ɋ K1 tbl on RS, p1 tbl on WS	⊐ 3-st TRKC
⟋ K2tog	⟍ 2-st TRPC	⊐ 3-st TLKC
⟍ Ssk	⟋ 2-st TLPC	

Make Bobble (MB) [K1, p1] twice into next st, turn, p4, turn, pass 2nd, 3rd and 4th sts over first st.

9-st RC Sl 5 sts to cn and hold to *back*, k4, k5 from cn.

(multiple of 28 sts plus 5)

Rows 1, 3, 5 and 7 (RS) K2, k2tog, *k5, yo, k1, yo, k5, SK2P; rep from *, end last rep SKP, k2 (instead of SK2P).

Rows 2, 4, 6 and 8 K9, *p1, k13; rep from *, end last rep k9 (instead of k13).

Row 9 K2, k2tog, *k3, yo, k2tog, yo, k1, yo, SKP, yo, k3, SK2P; rep from *, end last rep SKP, k2 (instead of SK2P).

Row 10 K6, *p7, k7; rep from *, end last rep k6 (instead of k7).

Row 11 K2, k2tog, *k2, yo, k2tog, [k1, yo] twice, k1, SKP, yo, k2, SK2P; rep from *, end last rep SKP, k2 (instead of SK2P).

Row 12 K5, *p9, k5; rep from * to end.

Row 13 K2, k2tog, *k1, yo, k2tog, k2, yo, k1, yo, k2, SKP, yo, k1, SK2P; rep from *, end last rep SKP, k2 (instead of SK2P).

Row 14 K4, *p11, k3; rep from * to last st, end k1.

Row 15 K2, k2tog, yo, *k1, SKP, k2, yo, k1, yo, k2, k2tog, k1, yo, SK2P, yo; rep from *, end last rep yo, SKP, k2 (instead of yo, SK2P, yo).

Row 16 K1, p3, k1, *p23, k1, p3, k1; rep from * to end.

Row 17 P1, k3, p1, *yo, SKP, k5, k2tog, yo, k5, yo, SKP, k5, k2tog, yo, p1, k3, p1; rep from * to end.

Row 18 K1, p3, k1, *k1, p21, k2, p3, k1; rep from * to end.

Row 19 P1, yo, S2KP, yo, p1, *p1, yo, SKP, k3, k2tog, yo, k7, yo, SKP, k3, k2tog, yo, p2, yo, S2KP, yo, p1; rep from * to end.

Row 20 K1, p3, k1, *k2, p19, k3, p3, k1; rep from * to end.

Row 21 P1, k3, p1, *p2, yo, SKP, k1, k2tog, yo, 9-st RC, yo, SKP, k1, k2tog, yo, p3, k3, p1; rep from * to end.

Rows 22–44 (even rows) K1, p3, k1, *k3, p3, k1, p9, k1, p3, k4, p3, k1; rep from * to end.

Row 23 P1, yo, S2KP, yo, p1, *p3, yo, S2KP, yo, p1, k9, p1, yo, S2KP, yo, p4, yo, S2KP, yo, p1; rep from * to end.

Row 25 P1, k3, p1, *p3, k3, p1, yo, SKP, k5, k2tog, yo, p1, k3, p4, k3, p1; rep from * to end.

Row 27 P1, yo, S2KP, yo, p1, *p3, yo, S2KP, yo, p1, k1, yo, SKP, k3, k2tog, yo, k1, p1, yo, S2KP, yo, p4, yo, S2KP, yo, p1; rep from * to end.

Row 29 P1, k3, p1, *p3, k3, p1, MB, k1, yo, SKP, k1, k2tog, yo, k1, MB, p1, k3, p4, k3, p1; rep from * to end.

Row 31 P1, yo, S2KP, yo, p1, *p3, yo, S2KP, yo, p1, k1, MB, k1, yo, S2KP, yo, k1, MB, k1, p1, yo, S2KP, yo, p4, yo, S2KP, yo, p1; rep from * to end.

Row 33 P1, k3, p1, *p3, k3, p1, k2, MB, k3, MB, k2, p1, k3, p4, k3, p1; rep from * to end.

Row 35 P1, yo, S2KP, yo, p1, *p3, yo, S2KP, yo, p1, k3, MB, k1, MB, k3, p1, yo, S2KP, yo, p4, yo, S2KP, yo, p1; rep from * to end.

Row 37 P1, k3, p1, *p3, k3, p1, k4, MB, k4, p1, k3, p4, k3, p1; rep from * to end.

Row 39 Rep row 23.

Row 41 P1, k3, p1, *p3, k3, p1, k9, p1, k3, p4, k3, p1; rep from * to end.

Row 43 Rep row 23.

Row 45 P1, k3, p1, *p3, k3, p1, 9-st RC, p1, k3, p4, k3, p1; rep from * to end.

Row 46 Rep row 22.

Rep rows 23–46.

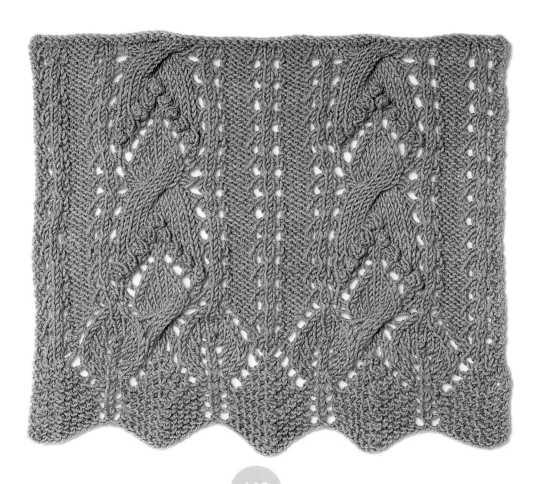

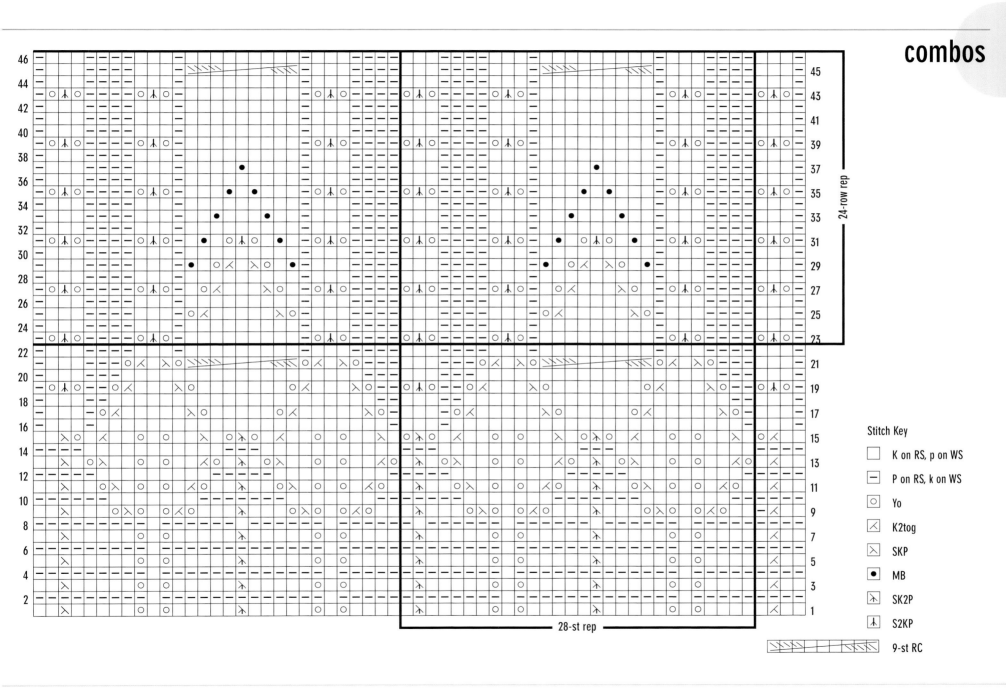

combos

Stitch Key

- ☐ K on RS, p on WS
- — P on RS, k on WS
- ○ Yo
- ╱ K2tog
- ╲ SKP
- • MB
- ⋏ SK2P
- ⟂ S2KP
- ⟍⟍⟍⟍ 9-st RC

(multiple of 24 sts plus 13)

Row 1 (RS) *K1 CC1, k4 MC, k3 CC1, k4 MC; rep from *, end k1 CC1.

Row 2 P2 CC1, *p2 MC, p1 CC1, p3 MC, p1 CC1, p2 MC, p3 CC1; rep from *, end last rep p2 (instead of 3) CC1.

Row 3 *K1 CC1, k2 MC; rep from *, end k1 CC1.

Row 4 P2 MC, p1 CC1, *p2 MC, p3 CC1, p2 MC, p1 CC1, p3 MC, p1 CC1; rep from * to last 10 sts, end p2 MC, p3 CC1, p2 MC, p1 CC1, p2 MC.

Row 5 K2 CC1, *k4 MC, k1 CC1, k4 MC, k3 CC1; rep from *, end last rep k2 (instead of 3) CC1.

Rows 6, 8, 10 12 and 14 With MC, purl.

Row 7 With MC, knit.

Rows 9 and 11 With MC, *k1, [k2tog] twice, [yo, k1] 3 times, yo, [ssk] twice; rep from *, end k1.

Row 13 With MC, knit.

Row 15 *K1 CC2, k1 MC, k1 CC2, k3 MC, k1 CC2, k3 MC, k1 CC2, k1 MC, k1 CC2, k4 MC, k3 CC2, k4 MC; rep from * to last 13 sts, end k1 CC2, k1 MC, k1 CC2, k3 MC, k1 CC2, k3 MC, k1 CC2, k1 MC, k1 CC2.

Row 16 *[P1 MC, p1 CC2] twice, p2 MC, p1 CC2, p2 MC, p1 CC2, p1 MC, p1 CC2, p4 MC, p5 CC2, p3 MC; rep from * to last 13 sts, end [p1 MC, p1 CC2] twice, p2 MC, p1 CC2, p2 MC, [p1 CC2, p1 MC] twice.

Row 17 *K2 MC, [k1 CC2, k1 MC] 4 times, k1 CC2, k4 MC, k2 CC2, k3 MC, k2 CC2, k2 MC; rep from * to last 13 sts, end k2 MC, [k1 CC2, k1 MC] 4 times, k1 CC2, k2 MC.

Row 18 *P1 CC2, p2 MC, p1 CC2, p1 MC, p3 CC2, p1 MC, p1 CC2, p2 MC, p3 CC2, p3 MC, p1 CC2, p3 MC, p2 CC2; rep from * to last 13 sts, end p1 CC2, p2 MC, p1 CC2, p1 MC, p3 CC2, p1 MC, p1 CC2, p2 MC, p1 CC2.

Row 19 *K3 CC2, k1 MC, k1 CC2, k3 MC, k1 CC2, k1 MC, k3 CC2, [k3 MC, k1 CC2] twice, k3 MC; rep from * to last 13 sts, end k3 CC2, k1 MC, k1 CC2, k3 MC, k1 CC2, k1 MC, k3 CC2.

Row 20 *[P3 CC1, p2 MC] twice, p3 CC1, p5 MC, p1 CC1, p5 MC; rep from * to last 13 sts, end [p3 CC1, p2 MC] twice, p3 CC1.

Row 21 *[K1 CC1, k5 MC] twice, k4 CC1, [k1 MC, k3 CC1] twice; rep from * to last 13 sts, end [k1 CC1, k5 MC] twice, k1 CC1.

Row 22 *[P3 MC, p2 CC2] twice, p6 MC, [p1 CC2, p1 MC] twice, p1 CC2, p3 MC; rep from * to last 13 sts, end [p3 MC, p2 CC2] twice, p3 MC.

Row 23 Rep row 21.

Row 24 Rep row 20.

Row 25 Rep row 19.

Row 26 Rep row 18.

Row 27 Rep row 17.

Row 28 Rep row 16.

Row 29 Rep row 15.

Rows 30–38 Rep rows 6–14.

Rep rows 1–38.

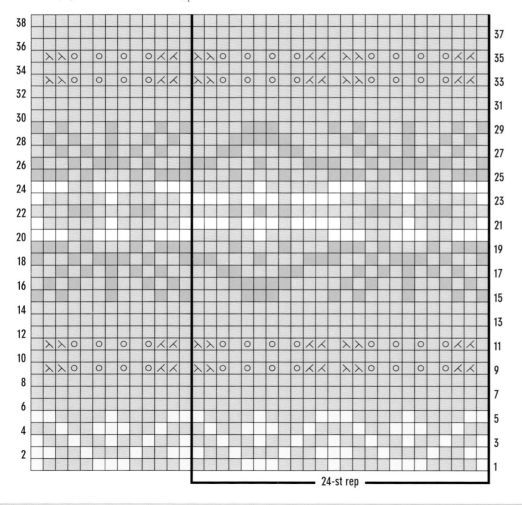

Stitch Key

☐ K on RS, p on WS

⊙ Yo

⟋ K2tog

⟍ Ssk

Color Key

▨ mc

☐ cc1

▨ cc2

☐ cc3

24-st rep

5-st RC Sl 3 sts to cn and hold to *back*, k2, k3 from cn.
(multiple of 20 sts plus 1)
Row 1 (RS) K3, *p2, k2tog, k3, yo, k1, yo, k3, ssk, p2, k5;
rep from *, end last rep k3 (instead of k5).
Row 2 and all WS rows P the purl sts and yos and k the
knit sts.
Row 3 K3, *p1, k2tog, [k3, yo] twice, k3, ssk, p1, 5-st RC;
rep from *, end last rep k3 (instead of 5-st RC).
Row 5 K3, *k2tog, k3, yo, k5, yo, k3, ssk, k5; rep from *,
end last rep k3 (instead of k5).

Row 7 K2, *k2tog, k3, yo, p1, k5, p1, yo, k3, ssk, k3; rep from
*, end last rep k2 (instead of k3).
Row 9 K1, *k2tog, k3, yo, p2, k5, p2, yo, k3, ssk, k1; rep from
* to end.
Row 11 Ssk, *k3, yo, p3, k5, p3, yo, k3, S2KP; rep from *, end
last rep k2tog (instead of S2KP).
Row 13 Ssk, *k2, yo, k1, p3, k5, p3, k1, yo, k2, S2KP; rep from
*, end last rep k2tog (instead of S2KP).
Row 15 Ssk, *k1, yo, k2, p3, 5-st RC, p3, k2, yo, k1, S2KP; rep
from *, end last rep k2tog (instead of S2KP).

Row 17 Ssk, *yo, k3, p3, k5, p3, k3, yo, S2KP; rep from *, end last
rep k2tog (instead of S2KP).
Row 19 K1, *yo, k3, ssk, p2, k5, p2, k2tog, k3, yo, k1; rep from *
to end.
Row 21 K2, *yo, k3, ssk, p1, 5-st RC, p1, k2tog, k3, yo, k3; rep
from *, end last rep k2 (instead of k3).
Row 23 K3, *yo, k3, ssk, k5, k2tog, k3, yo, k5; rep from *, end last
rep k3 (instead of k5).
Row 25 K3, *p1, yo, k3, ssk, k3, k2tog, k3, yo, p1, k5; rep from *,
end last rep k3 (instead of k5).
Row 27 K3, *p2, yo, k3, ssk, k1, k2tog, k3, yo, p2, 5-st RC; rep
from *, end last rep k3 (instead of 5-st RC).
Row 29 K3, *p3, yo, k3, S2KP, k3, yo, p3, k5; rep from *, end last
rep k3 (instead of k5).
Row 31 K3, *p3, k1, yo, k2, S2KP, k2, yo, k1, p3, k5; rep from *,
end last rep k3 (instead of k5).
Row 33 K3, *p3, k2, yo, k1, S2KP, k1, yo, k2, p3, 5-st RC; rep from
*, end last rep k3 (instead of 5-st RC).
Row 35 K3, *p3, k3, yo, S2KP, yo, k3, p3, k5; rep from *, end last
rep k3 (instead of k5).
Row 36 Rep row 2.
Rep rows 1–36.

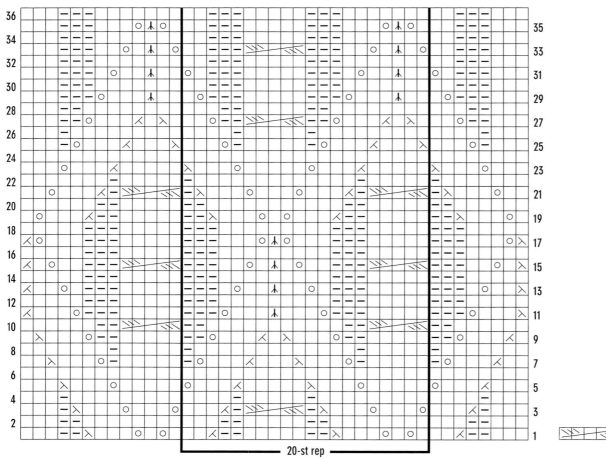

20-st rep

Stitch Key

☐	K on RS, p on WS
▭	P on RS, k on WS
⊙	Yo
◹	K2tog
◺	Ssk
⅄	S2KP
⧄⧄	5-st RC

(multiple of 20 sts)
Row 1 (RS) *K5, [k2tog, yo] 5 times, k5; rep from * to end.
Row 2 Purl.
Rep rows 1–2.
Work embroidery as desired in St st panels.

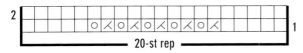

Stitch Key

☐ K on RS, p on WS

⊡ Yo

◹ K2tog

152

motifs

153 french swirl

Cast on 8 sts and distribute evenly over 4 dpns.
Place marker and join, taking care not to twist sts.
Work as foll, changing to circular needle when sts
no longer fit on dpns.
Rnds 1 and 2 Knit.
Rnd 3 [Yo, k1] 8 times—16 sts.
Rnd 4 Knit.
Rnd 5 [Yo, k1] 16 times—32 sts.
Rnd 6 [K2, k2tog] 8 times—24 sts.
Rnd 7 [Yo, k1, yo, k2tog] 8 times—32 sts.
Rnd 8 Knit.
Rnd 9 [(Yo, k1) twice, yo, k2tog] 8 times—48 sts.
Rnd 10 [K4, k2tog] 8 times—40 sts.
Rnd 11 [(Yo, k1) 3 times, k2tog] 8 times—56 sts.
Rnd 12 [K5, k2tog] 8 times—48 sts.
Rnd 13 [(Yo, k1) twice, yo, k2, k2tog] 8 times—64 sts.
Rnd 14 [K6, k2tog] 8 times—56 sts.
Rnd 15 [(Yo, k1) twice, yo, k3, k2tog] 8 times—72 sts.
Rnd 16 [K7, k2tog] 8 times—64 sts.
Rnd 17 [(Yo, k1) twice, yo, k4, k2tog] 8 times—80 sts.
Rnd 18 [K8, k2tog] 8 times—72 sts.

Rnd 19 [(Yo, k1) twice, yo, k5, k2tog] 8 times—88 sts.
Rnd 20 [K9, k2tog] 8 times—80 sts.
Rnd 21 [(Yo, k1) twice, yo, k6, k2tog] 8 times—96 sts.
Rnd 22 [K10, k2tog] 8 times—88 sts.
Rnd 23 [(Yo, k1) twice, yo, k7, k2tog] 8 times—104 sts.
Rnd 24 [K11, k2tog] 8 times—96 sts.
Rnd 25 [(Yo, k1) twice, yo, k8, k2tog] 8 times—112 sts.
Rnd 26 [K12, k2tog] 8 times—104 sts.
Rnd 27 [(Yo, k1) twice, yo, k9, k2tog] 8 times—120 sts.
Rnd 28 [K13, k2tog] 8 times—112 sts.
Rnd 29 [(Yo, k1) twice, yo, k10, k2tog] 8 times—128 sts.
Rnd 30 [K14, k2tog] 8 times—120 sts.
Rnd 31 [(Yo, k1) twice, yo, k11, k2tog] 8 times—136 sts.
Rnd 32 [K15, k2tog] 8 times—128 sts.
Rnd 33 [(Yo, k1) twice, yo, k12, k2tog] 8 times—144 sts.
Rnd 34 [K16, k2tog] 8 times—136 sts.
Rnd 35 [(Yo, k1) twice, yo, k13, k2tog] 8 times—152 sts.
Rnd 36 [K17, k2tog] 8 times—144 sts.
Rnds 37-39 Purl.
Bind off knitwise.

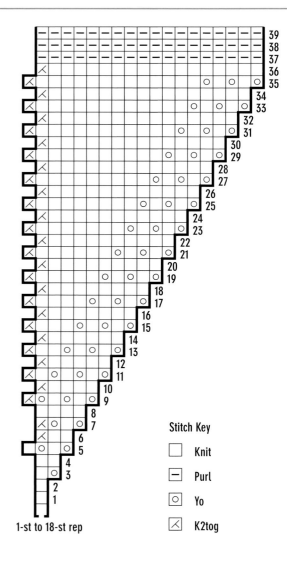

Stitch Key

☐	Knit
⊟	Purl
⊙	Yo
⊠	K2tog

1-st to 18-st rep

154 ferris wheel

With circular needle, cast on 96 sts. Place marker and join, taking care not to twist sts. Work as foll, changing to dpns when sts no longer fit on circular needle.

Rnd 1 Knit.
Rnd 2 *K2tog, k12, SKP; rep from * around—84 sts.
Rnd 3 *Yo, p2tog; rep from * around.
Rnd 4 Knit.
Rnd 5 *K2tog, k10, SKP; rep from * around—72 sts.
Rnd 6 *K2tog, yo twice, SKP; rep from * around.
Rnd 7 *K5, k1 into first yo, p1 into 2nd yo, k5; rep from * around.
Rnd 8 *K2tog, [yo, SKP, k2tog, yo] twice, SKP;
rep from * around—60 sts.

Rnd 9 *K4, k1 into first yo, p1 into first yo, k4; rep from * around.
Rnd 10 *K3, k2tog, yo twice, SKP, k3; rep from * around.
Rnd 11 *K2tog, k2, k1 into first yo, p1 into first yo, k2, SKP—48 sts.
Rnd 12 *K2, k2tog, yo twice, SKP, k2; rep from * around.
Rnd 13 *K3, k1 into first yo, p1 into 2nd yo, k3; rep from * around.
Rnd 14 *[K2tog] twice, yo twice, [SKP] twice—36 sts.
Rnd 15 *K2, k1 into first yo, p1 into 2nd yo, k2; rep from * around.
Rnd 16 Knit.
Rnds 17–20 *Yo, p2tog; rep from * around.
Cut yarn, leaving a 12"/30.5cm tail. Thread yarn through sts and pull tightly to close.

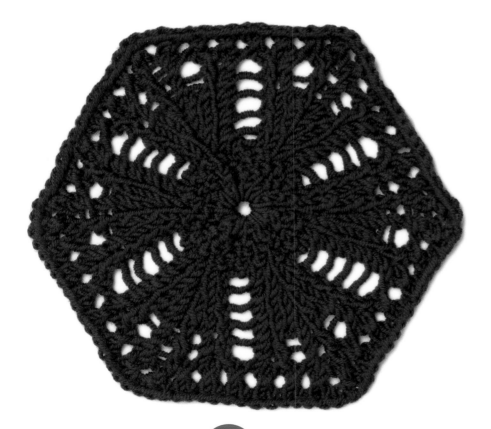

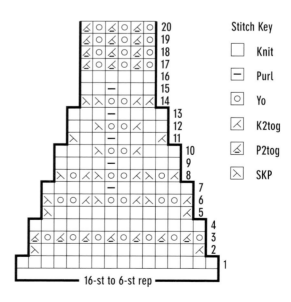

Stitch Key

☐ Knit

— Purl

○ Yo

⊿ K2tog

⊿ P2tog

⊠ SKP

16-st to 6-st rep

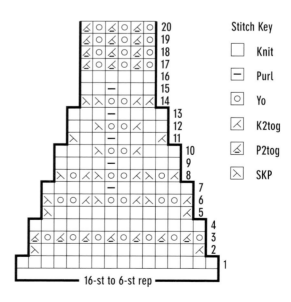

155 pinwheel

With dpn, cast on 3 sts. K 1 row. Distribute sts over 3 dpns, place marker and join. Work as foll, changing to circular needle when sts no longer fit on dpns.

Rnd 1 and all odd rnds Knit. (**Note** On rnds above double and triple yos, work yos as 1 st, dropping extra loops.)

Rnd 2 [Yo, k1] 3 times—6 sts.
Rnd 4 [Yo, k1] 6 times—12 sts.
Rnd 6 [Yo twice, k1] 12 times—24 sts.
Rnd 8 [Yo twice, k4] 6 times—30 sts.
Rnd 10 [Yo twice, k5] 6 times—36 sts.

Rnd 12 [Yo 3 times, k6] 6 times—42 sts.
Rnd 14 [Yo 3 times, k7] 6 times—48 sts.
Rnd 16 [Yo 3 times, k8] 6 times—54 sts.
Rnd 18 [Yo 3 times, k1, yo 3 times, ssk, k6] 6 times—60 sts.
Rnd 20 [Yo 3 times, k3, yo 3 times, ssk, k5] 6 times—66 sts.
Rnd 22 [Yo 3 times, k5, yo 3 times, ssk, k4] 6 times—72 sts.
Rnd 24 [Yo 3 times, k7, yo 3 times, ssk, k3] 6 times—78 sts.
Rnd 26 [Yo 3 times, k9, yo 3 times, ssk, k2] 6 times—84 sts.
Rnd 28 [Yo 3 times, k11, yo 3 times, ssk, k1] 6 times—90 sts.
Rnd 29 Knit.
Bind off loosely.

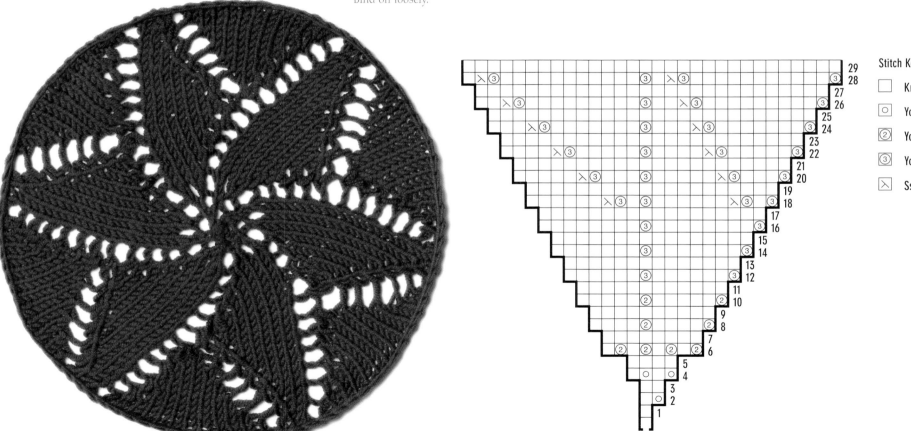

Stitch Key

☐ Knit
○ Yo
② Yo twice
③ Yo 3 times
⋉ Ssk

1-st to 30-st rep

155

156 sea star

Inc 2 [K1, yo, k1] into a st—3 sts.
Make a sl knot and place on dpn. With 2nd dpn, [k1, p1] 6 times into sl knot—12 sts. Distribute sts evenly over 3 dpns. Place marker, join and work as foll, changing to circular needle when sts no longer fit on dpns.
Rnd 1 and all odd rnds Knit.
Rnd 2 [Yo, k1] 12 times—24 sts.
Rnd 4 [K2, inc 2, k1] 6 times—36 sts.
Rnd 6 [K3, inc 2, k2] 6 times—48 sts.
Rnd 8 [K4, inc 2, k3] 6 times—60 sts.
Rnd 10 [K5, inc 2, k4] 6 times—72 sts.
Rnd 12 [K6, inc 2, k5] 6 times—84 sts.
Rnd 14 [K7, inc 2, k6] 6 times—96 sts.
Rnd 16 [K1, yo, ssk, k11, k2tog, yo] 6 times.
Rnd 18 [(K1, yo) twice, ssk, k9, k2tog, yo, k1, yo] 6 times—108 sts.
Rnd 20 [K1, yo, k2tog, yo, k1, yo, ssk, k7, (k2tog, yo) twice, k1, yo] 6 times—120 sts.
Rnd 22 [K1, yo, (k2tog, yo) twice, k1, yo, ssk, k5, (k2tog, yo) 3 times, k1, yo] 6 times—132 sts.
Rnd 24 [K1, yo, (k2tog, yo) 3 times, k1, yo, ssk, k3, (k2tog, yo) 4 times, k1, yo] 6 times—144 sts.
Rnd 26 [K1, yo, (k2tog, yo) 4 times, k1, yo, ssk, k1,

(k2tog, yo) 5 times, k1, yo] 6 times—156 sts.
Rnd 28 [K1, yo, (k2tog, yo) 5 times, k1, yo, S2KP, yo, (k2tog, yo) 5 times, k1, yo] 6 times—168 sts.
Rnd 30 [K1, yo, (k2tog, yo) 13 times, k1, yo] 6 times—180 sts.
Rnd 32 [K1, yo, k29, yo] 6 times—192 sts.
Next rnd Bind off as foll: K1, *yo, k1, sl first k st and yo up and over last st and off needle; rep from * around.

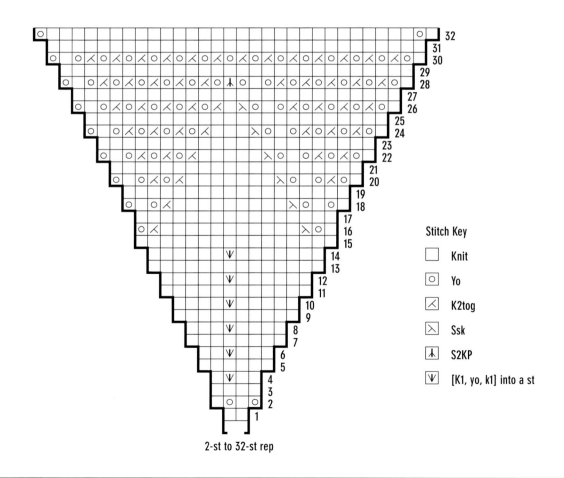

2-st to 32-st rep

Stitch Key

☐	Knit
⊙	Yo
╱	K2tog
╲	Ssk
⋏	S2KP
Ψ	[K1, yo, k1] into a st

156

157 botanica medallion

Cast on 6 sts, leaving an 8"/20.5 cm tail (for working center knob later) and distribute sts evenly over 3 dpns. Place marker and join, taking care not to twist sts. Work as foll, changing to circular needle when sts no longer fit on dpns.
Rnds 1, 3, 5 and 7 Knit.
Rnd 2 [(K1, yo, k1) into a st] 6 times—18 sts.
Rnd 4 [(K1, yo) twice, k1] 6 times—30 sts.
Rnd 6 [K2, yo, k1, yo, k2] 6 times—42 sts.
Rnd 8 [K2, p1, yo, k1, yo, p1, k2] 6 times—54 sts.
Rnds 9 and 11 [K2, p1, k3, p1, k2] 6 times.
Rnd 10 [K1, ssk, p1, yo, k1, yo, p1, k2tog, k1] 6 times.
Rnd 12 [K2, p2, yo, k1, yo, p2, k2] 6 times—66 sts.
Rnds 13 and 15 [K2, p2, k3, p2, k2] 6 times.
Rnd 14 [K1, ssk, p2, yo, k1, yo, p2, k2tog, k1] 6 times.
Rnd 16 [K2, p3, yo, k1, yo, p3, k2] 6 times—78 sts.
Rnds 17 and 19 [K2, p3, k3, p3, k2] 6 times.
Rnd 18 [K1, ssk, p3, yo, k1, yo, p3, k2tog, k1] 6 times.
Rnd 20 [K2, p4, yo, k1, yo, p4, k2] 6 times—90 sts.
Rnds 21 and 23 [K2, p4, k3, p4, k2] 6 times.
Rnd 22 [K1, ssk, p4, yo, k1, yo, p4, k2tog, k1] 6 times.
Rnd 24 [K2, p5, yo, k1, yo, p5, k2] 6 times—102 sts.
Rnd 25 [K2, p5, k3, p5, k2] 6 times.
Rnd 26 [Yo, k1, ssk, p5, yo, k1, yo, p5, k2tog, k1] 6 times—108 sts.
Rnd 27 [(K3, p5) twice, k2] 6 times.
Rnd 28 [(Yo, k1) twice, ssk, p11, k2tog, k1] 6 times.
Rnd 29 [K5, p11, k2] 6 times.
Rnd 30 [Yo, k3, yo, k2, p11, k2] 6 times—120 sts.
Rnd 31 [K7, p11, k2] 6 times.
Rnd 32 [Yo, k5, yo, k1, ssk, p9, k2tog, k1] 6 times.

Rnd 33 [K9, p9, k2] 6 times.
Rnd 34 [Yo, k7, yo, k2, p9, k2] 6 times—132 sts.
Rnd 35 [K11, p9, k2] 6 times.
Rnd 36 [Yo, k3, yo, SK2P, yo, k3, yo, k1, ssk, p7, k2tog, k1] 6 times.
Rnd 37 [K13, p7, k2] 6 times.
Rnd 38 [Yo, k3, yo, k1, SK2P, k1, yo, k3, yo, k2, p7, k2] 6 times—144 sts.
Rnd 39 [K15, p7, k2] 6 times.
Rnd 40 [Yo, k3, yo, k2, SK2P, k2, yo, k3, yo, k1, ssk, p5, k2tog, k1] 6 times.
Rnd 41 [K17, p5, k2] 6 times.
Rnd 42 [(Yo, k3) twice, SK2P, (k3, yo) twice, k2, p5, k2] 6 times—156 sts.
Rnd 43 [K19, p5, k2] 6 times.
Rnd 44 [Yo, k3, yo, k4, SK2P, k4, yo, k3, yo, k1, ssk, p3, k2tog, k1] 6 times.
Rnd 45 [K21, p3, k2] 6 times.
Rnd 46 [Yo, k3, yo, k5, SK2P, k5, yo, k3, yo, k2, p3, k2] 6 times—168 sts.
Rnd 47 [K23, p3, k2] 6 times.
Rnd 48 [Yo, k3, yo, k6, SK2P, k6, yo, k3, yo, k1, ssk, p1, k2tog, k1] 6 times.
Rnd 49 [K25, p1, k2] 6 times.
Rnd 50 [Yo, k3, yo, k7, SK2P, k7, yo, k3, yo, k2, p1, k2] 6 times—180 sts.
Rnd 51 [K27, p1, k2] 6 times.
Rnd 52 [Yo, k3, yo, k8, SK2P, k8, yo, k3, yo, k1, SK2P, k1] 6 times.
Rnd 53 Knit.
Rnd 54 [Yo, k3, yo, k9, SK2P, k9, (yo, k3) twice] 6 times—192 sts.
Rnd 55 Knit.
Bind off.
Center knob Make a knob in center of motif as foll: With RS facing and tapestry needle, weave cast-on tail through sts of rnd 3. Pull yarn tightly to form knob. Go around once more, weaving in and out of every other st. Bring tail to WS and secure.

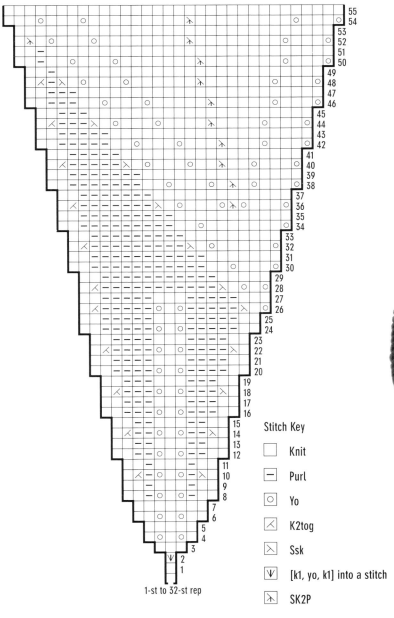

Row numbers (right side of chart, bottom to top): 1, 2, 3, 4, 5, 6, 7, 8, 9, 10, 11, 12, 13, 14, 15, 16, 17, 18, 19, 20, 21, 22, 23, 24, 25, 26, 27, 28, 29, 30, 31, 32, 33, 34, 35, 36, 37, 38, 39, 40, 41, 42, 43, 44, 45, 46, 47, 48, 49, 50, 51, 52, 53, 54, 55

1-st to 32-st rep

Stitch Key

☐	Knit
−	Purl
○	Yo
⟋	K2tog
⟍	Ssk
⟱	[k1, yo, k1] into a stitch
⟑	SK2P

157

158 dos equis

3-to-2 dec Sl 1 knitwise wyib, k2, psso.
(multiple of 30 sts plus 5)
Row 1 (RS) K1, yo, SK2P, yo, *k3, yo, ssk, k4, yo, SSSK, yo, k3, yo, k3tog, yo, k4, k2tog, yo, k3, yo, SK2P, yo; rep from *, end k1.
Row 2 and all WS rows K1, p to last st, k1.
Row 3 K4, *yo, SK2P, yo, k1, yo, ssk, k4, yo, ssk, yo, SK2P, yo, k2tog, yo, k4, k2tog, yo, k1, yo, SK2P, yo, k3; rep from *, end k1.
Row 5 K1, yo, SK2P, yo, *k3, [yo, ssk] twice, k4, yo, ssk, k1, k2tog, yo, k4, [k2tog, yo] twice, k3, yo, SK2P, yo; rep from *, end k1.
Row 7 K4, *yo, SK2P, yo, k3, yo, ssk, k4, yo, 3-to-2 dec, yo, k4, k2tog, yo, k3, yo, SK2P, yo, k3; rep from *, end k1.
Row 9 K1, yo, SK2P, yo, *k3, yo, SK2P, yo, k1, yo, ssk, k3, k2tog, yo, ssk, k3, k2tog, yo, k1, yo, SK2P, yo, k3, yo, SK2P, yo; rep from *, end k1.
Row 11 K4, *yo, SSSK, yo, k3, [yo, ssk] twice, k7, [k2tog, yo] twice, k3, yo, k3tog, yo, k3; rep from *, end k1.
Row 13 K4, *k1, yo, ssk, yo, SK2P, yo, k3, yo, ssk, k5, k2tog, yo, k3, yo, SK2P, yo, k2tog, yo, k4; rep from *, end k1.

Row 15 K4, *k2, yo, ssk, k2, yo, SK2P, yo, k1, yo, ssk, k3, k2tog, yo, k1, yo, SK2P, yo, k2, k2tog, yo, k5; rep from *, end k1.
Row 17 K4, *k3, yo, SSSK, yo, k3, [yo, ssk] twice, k1, [k2tog, yo] twice, k3, yo, k3tog, yo, k6; rep from *, end k1.
Row 19 K2, yo, ssk, *k4, yo, ssk, [yo, SK2P, yo, k3] twice, yo, SK2P, yo, k2tog, yo, k5, yo, ssk; rep from *, end k1.
Row 21 K3, *yo, ssk, k4, yo, ssk, k2, yo, SK2P, yo, k3, yo, SK2P, yo, k2, k2tog, yo, k4, k2tog, yo, k1; rep from *, end k2.
Row 23 K4, *yo, ssk, k4, yo, SSSK, yo, k3, yo, SK2P, yo, k3, yo, k3tog, yo, k4, k2tog, yo, k3; rep from *, end k1.
Row 25 K1, yo, SK2P, yo, *k1, yo, ssk, k4, yo, ssk, yo, SK2P, yo, k3, yo, SK2P, yo, k2tog, yo, k4, k2tog, yo, k1, yo, SK2P, yo; rep from *, end k1.
Row 27 K4, *[yo, ssk] twice, k4, yo, ssk, k2, yo, SK2P, yo, k2, k2tog, yo, k4, [k2tog, yo] twice, k3; rep from *, end k1.
Row 29 K1, yo, SK2P, yo, *k3, yo, ssk, k4, yo, SSSK, yo, k3, yo, k3tog, yo, k4, k2tog, yo, k3, yo, SK2P, yo; rep from *, end k1.

Row 31 K4, *yo, k3tog, yo, k4, k2tog, yo, k3, yo, SK2P, yo, k3, yo, ssk, k4, yo, SSSK, yo, k3; rep from *, end k1.
Row 33 K1, yo, SK2P, yo, *k2tog, yo, k4, k2tog, yo, k1, yo, SK2P, yo, k3, yo, SK2P, yo, k1, yo, ssk, k4, yo, ssk, yo, SK2P, yo; rep from *, end k1.
Row 35 K3, *k2tog, yo, k4, [k2tog, yo] twice, k3, yo, SK2P, yo, k3, [yo, ssk] twice, k4, yo, ssk, k1; rep from *, end k2.
Row 37 K1, yo, 3-to-2 dec, yo, *k4, k2tog, yo, [k3, yo, SK2P, yo] twice, k3, yo, ssk, k4, yo, 3-to-2 dec , yo; rep from *, end k1.
Row 39 K1, k2tog, yo, ssk, *k3, k2tog, yo, k1, [yo, SK2P, yo, k3] twice, yo, SK2P, yo, k1, yo, ssk, k3, k2tog, yo, ssk; rep from *, end k1.
Row 41 K4, *k2, [k2tog, yo] twice, k3, yo, k3tog, yo, k3, yo, SSSK, yo, k3, [yo, ssk] twice, k5; rep from *, end k1.
Row 43 K4, *k1, k2tog, yo, k3, yo, SK2P, yo, k2tog, yo, k5, yo, ssk, yo, SK2P, yo, k3, yo, ssk, k4; rep from *, end k1.
Row 45 K4, *k2tog, yo, k1, yo, SK2P, yo, k2, k2tog, yo, k7, yo, ssk, k2, yo, SK2P, yo, k1, yo, ssk, k3; rep from *, end k1.
Row 47 K3, *[k2tog, yo] twice, k3, yo, k3tog, yo, k9, yo, SSSK, yo, k3, [yo, ssk] twice, k1; rep from *, end k2.
Row 49 K1, yo, SK2P, yo, *k3, yo, SK2P, yo, k2tog, yo, k5, yo, ssk, k4, yo, ssk, yo, SK2P, yo, k3, yo, SK2P, yo; rep from * end k1.
Row 51 K4, *yo, SK2P, yo, k2, k2tog, yo, k4, k2tog, yo, k1, yo, ssk, k4, yo, ssk, k2, yo, SK2P, yo, k3; rep from *, end k1.
Row 53 K1, yo, SK2P, yo, *k3, yo, k3tog, yo, k4, k2tog, yo, k3, yo, ssk, k4, yo, SSSK, yo, k3, yo, SK2P, yo; rep from *, end k1.
Row 55 K4, *yo, SK2P, yo, k2tog, yo, k4, k2tog, yo, k1, yo, SK2P, yo, k1, yo, ssk, k4, yo, ssk, yo, SK2P, yo, k3; rep from *, end k1.
Row 57 K1, yo, SK2P, yo, *k2, k2tog, yo, k4, [k2tog, yo] twice, k3, [yo, ssk] twice, k4, yo, ssk, k2, yo, SK2P, yo; rep from *, end k1.
Row 59 K4, *yo, k3tog, yo, k4, k2tog, yo, k3, yo, SK2P, yo, k3, yo, ssk, k4, yo, SSSK, yo, k3; rep from *, end k1.
Row 60 K1, p to last st, k1.
Rep rows 1–60.

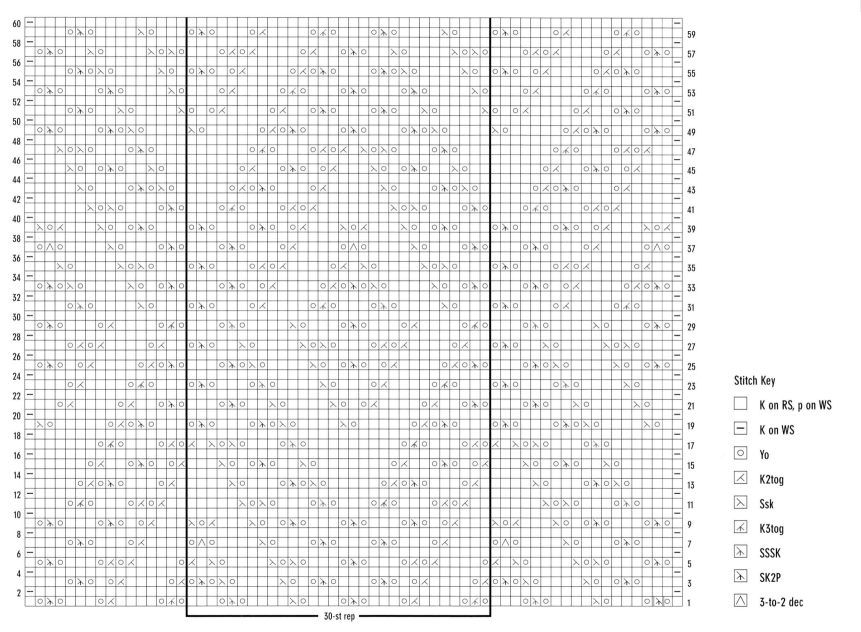

Stitch Key

☐	K on RS, p on WS
—	K on WS
○	Yo
╱	K2tog
╲	Ssk
⋏	K3tog
⋏	SSSK
⋏	SK2P
⋀	3-to-2 dec

30-st rep

abbreviations

petticoats p. 36

approx—approximately

beg—begin; begins; beginning

CC—contrasting color

cn—cable needle

cont—continue; continuing

dec—decrease; decreasing

dpn—double-pointed needle

inc—increase; increasing

k—knit

k-b; k1-b—knit stitch in row below

k2tog—knit two together

k3tog—knit three together

LH—left-hand

lp; lps—loop; loops

MC—main color

m1—make one

m1 p-st—make one purl stitch

p—purl

pat; pats—pattern; patterns

pm—place marker

psso—pass slip stitch over

p2tog—purl two together

p3tog—purl three together

rem—remain; remaining

rep—repeat

RH—right-hand

RS—right side

SKP—slip one, knit one, pass slip stitch over

SK2P—slip one, knit two together, pass slip stitch over

S2KP—slip two stitches together, knit one, pass two slip stitches over

sl—slip

sm—slip marker

ssk—slip, slip, knit

ssp—slip, slip, purl

sssk—slip, slip, slip, knit

st; sts—stitch; stitches

St st—stockinette stitch

tbl—through back loop

tog—together

WS—wrong side

wyib—with yarn in back

wyif—with yarn in front

yo—yarn over

yo twice; yo2—yarn over two times

stained glass windows p. 19

teepees p. 64

chinese fans p. 78

caterpillar p. 131

cables and diamonds p. 158

sea star p. 166

Yarn overs

1. Between two knit stitches

Bring the yarn from the back of the work to the front between the two needles. Knit the next stitch, bringing the yarn to the back over the right needle as shown.

2. Between two purl stitches

Leave the yarn at the front of the work. Bring the yarn to the back over the right needle and to the front again as shown. Purl the next stitch.

3. Between a knit and a purl stitch

Bring the yarn from the back to the front between the two needles, then to the back over the right needle and to the front again as shown. Purl the next stitch.

4. Between a purl and a knit stitch

Leave the yarn at the front of the work. Knit the next stitch, bringing the yarn to the back over the right needle as shown.

5. At the beginning of a knit row

Keep the yarn at the front of the work. Insert the right needle knitwise into the first stitch on the left needle. Bring the yarn over the right needle to the back and knit the next stitch, holding the yarn over with your thumb if necessary.

6. At the beginning of a purl row

To work a yarn over at the beginning of a purl row, keep the yarn at the back of the work. Insert the right needle purlwise into the first stitch on the left needle. Purl the stitch.

7. Multiple yarn overs

a. For multiple yarn overs (two or more), wrap the yarn around the needle as for a single yarn over, then wrap the yarn around the needle once more (or as many times as indicated). Work the next stitch on the left needle.

b. Alternate knitting and purling into the multiple yarn over on the subsequent row, always knitting the last stitch on a purl row and purling the last stitch on a knit row.

glossary

as foll Work the instructions that follow.

end last rep After completing a full repeat of a pattern and not enough stitches remain to complete another repeat, end the pattern repeat as directed.

hold to front (back) of work A term usually referring to stitches placed on a cable needle that are held to the front (or the back) of the work as it faces you.

k the knit sts and p the purl sts (as they face you) A phrase used when a pattern of knit and purl stitches has been established and will continue for a determined length (such as ribbing). Work the stitches as they face you: Knit the knit stitches and purl the purl stitches.

k the purl sts and p the knit sts A phrase used when a pattern of knit and purl stitches will alternate on the following row or rows (such as in a seed stitch pattern). Work the stitches opposite of how they face you: Purl the knit stitches and knit the purl stitches.

knitwise (or as to knit) Insert the needle into the stitch as if you were going to knit it.

m1 Make one knit stitch as follows: Insert left needle from front to back under horizontal strand between stitch just worked and next stitch on left needle. Knit this strand through the back loop.

m1 p-st Make one purl stitch as follows: Insert left needle from front to back under horizontal strand between stitch just worked and next stitch on left needle. Purl this strand through the back loop.

multiple of . . . sts Used when working a pattern. The total number of stitches should be divisible by the number of stitches in one pattern repeat.

multiple of . . . sts plus . . . Used when working a pattern. The total number of stitches should be divisible by the number of stitches in one pattern repeat, plus the extra stitches (added only once).

next row (RS), or (WS) The row following the one just worked will be a right side (or wrong side) row.

place marker(s) Slide a stitch marker either onto the needle (where it is slipped every row) or attach it to a stitch, where it remains as a guide.

preparation row A row that sets up the stitch pattern but is not part of the pattern repeat.

purlwise Insert the needle into the stitch as if you were going to purl it.

rep from *, end . . . Repeat the instructions that begin at the asterisk as many times as you can work full repeats of the pattern, then end the row as directed.

rep from * to end Repeat the instructions that begin at the asterisk, ending the row with a full repeat of the pattern.

rep . . . times more Repeat a direction the designated number of times (not counting the first time you work it).

right side (or RS) Usually refers to the surface of the work that will face outside when the garment is worn.

row 2 and all WS (even-numbered) rows A term used when all the wrong-side or even-numbered rows are worked the same.

SKP On RS, slip one stitch. Knit next stitch and pass slip stitch over knit stitch. On WS, slip next two

stitches knitwise. Slip these two stitches back to left needle without twisting them and purl them together through the back loops.

SK2P On RS, slip one stitch, knit two stitches together. Pass slipped stitch over two stitches knit together. On WS, slip two stitches to right needle as if knitting two together. Slip next stitch knitwise. Slip all stitches to left needle without twisting them. Purl these three stitches together through back loops.

slip marker To keep the stitch marker in the same position from one row to the next, transfer it from one needle to the other as you work each row.

ssk On RS, slip next two stitches knitwise. Insert tip of left needle into fronts of these two stitches and knit them together. On WS, slip one stitch, purl one stitch, then pass slip stitch over purl stitch.

stockinette stitch Knit every right-side row and purl every wrong-side row.

work to end Work the established pattern to the end of the row.

acknowledgments

Special thanks to:

The Knitters:
Bonnie Arnold
Joni Coniglio
Amber Donahue
Mary Lou Eastman
Mary Ellen Meisters
Tana Pageler
Kelly Rokke
Leslie Terry
Carol Thompson
Meredith Wachter

And also:
Salli Sternberg

All yarn provided by:
Filatura Di Crosa
Distributed by Tahki • Stacy Charles, Inc.
70-30 80th Street, Building #36
Ridgewood, NY 11385
www.tahkistacycharles.com

hand in hand p. 149

Knitting needles on cover provided by Lantern Moon.

Lantern Moon knitting needles are currently available in four distinct wood varieties.

Made entirely by hand, they are the perfect tool for knitters. The design detail and handfinishing

make these needles as wonderful to work with as they are beautiful. Visit Lantern Moon online at

www.lanternmoon.com.

index